LIGHT ON C. S. LEWIS

LIGHT ON C. S. LEWIS

by

OWEN BARFIELD
AUSTIN FARRER
J. A. W. BENNETT
NEVILL COGHILL
JOHN LAWLOR
STELLA GIBBONS
KATHLEEN RAINE
CHAD WALSH
WALTER HOOPER

EDITED BY JOCELYN GIBB

GEOFFREY BLES · LONDON

1965

© Geoffrey Bles Ltd, 1965

Printed in Great Britain
by Richard Clay (The Chaucer Press), Ltd
Bungay, Suffolk
and published by
GEOFFREY BLES LTD
52 Doughty Street, London, W.C.1
33 York Street, Sydney
531 Little Collins Street, Melbourne
70–2 Eagle Street, Brisbane
CML Building, King William Street, Adelaide
Lake Road, Northcote, Auckland
10 Dyas Road, Don Mills, Ontario
P.O. Box 8879, Johannesburg
P.O. Box 834, Cape Town
P.O. Box 2800, Salisbury, Rhodesia

CONTENTS

45735

PREFACE

WHY SHOULD C. S. Lewis, who died two years ago at the age of sixty-five, need any light thrown on him? Was he a mystery man who hid himself away in the cloisters of a university, lecturing, tutoring and writing? Far from it; but there must inevitably be thousands of readers of his books who wonder what sort of man he was.

This book is no biography. All it does is to present, from several people who knew him and his writings, an answer to the simple question 'C. S. Lewis—how did he strike you?' A man with such a diversity of subjects, with such a wide-ranging, adventurous outlook, might well elicit conflicting views of him. But not a bit of it. Even with a certain amount of overlapping, which was deliberate and inevitable, we find a composite picture of very much a whole man, one with a closely knit mind and certainly not divided up into categorical departments. That he had several characteristics, and depths in them, which were hard to understand is perfectly true; and here again the following pages cite some of the resulting paradoxes. Yet the contributors were invited to show the man in the round as they found him and knew him and it is hoped that readers will feel, as I do, that they have been successful.

Professor Coghill, searching for the right word, depicts Lewis as 'formidable'. That is a very good description. Within it I found something else. It was his certainty, his sureness. That is not to say that he was superior or arrogant (though in argument he could sometimes throw you in the dust rather sharply), he had much too much of a sense of fun for that. It was simply that in all he took on he was sure of himself. He would adjust his mind ahead, rapidly and incisively, just as a fencer instinctively puts his feet in the right place, the correct amount of weight on each foot and the foil balanced to precision before he engages his opponent. And Lewis always took very good care that he performed or contested on ground of his own choosing. Of course behind it all he had the advantage of a scholarly mind (nurtured on the classics), a remarkable memory and above all an unshakable, deep sense of truth.

To give readers a very brief record: C. S. Lewis was born in Belfast in 1898, his father being a solicitor and his mother the daughter of a clergyman named Hamilton. 'My father's people,' he wrote in his autobiography, *Surprised by Joy,* 'were true Welshmen, sentimental, passionate and rhetorical, easily moved to anger and to tenderness; men who laughed and cried a great deal and who had not much of the talent for happiness. The Hamiltons were a cooler race. Their minds were critical and ironic and they had the talent for happiness in a high degree.' There were two children, both sons, the younger by three years being our subject and the elder W. H., who was his companion all his life.

C. S. Lewis (known as Jack to his family and friends) went to Malvern for a time and was afterwards educated privately. He was then elected a scholar of University College, Oxford in 1916, but went to France and 'arrived in the front line trenches on my nineteenth birthday (November 1917)'. Soon he was wounded and returned to Oxford, where he remained as a student and, from 1925, tutor at Magdalen, until 1954 when he moved to Cambridge and assumed a newly created chair of Medieval and Renaissance English, becoming a Fellow of Magdalene. He had just vacated that chair and fellowship, because of illness, when he died.

If the reader has no starting acquaintance with Lewis, either personally or through his works, then perhaps the introduction might better be read at the end. Finally I should just allude to two pieces of 'Lewisiana', one past, one future. For some time he had been thinking of collecting an edition of his poems and it was sad that this was never accomplished in his lifetime. However, Walter Hooper put them together and they were happily launched last year. Now this present book, *Light on C. S. Lewis*, is something of a prologue to *The Letters of C. S. Lewis*, which his brother has edited and which will appear in the earlier part of 1966.

My thanks are many and great, largely to: Owen Barfield for his help and encouragement and likewise to W. H. Lewis, Spencer Curtis Brown and Billy and Pierre Collins; to Nevill Coghill, John Lawlor, and Milton Waldman for manifold kindnesses; from R. W. Ladborough who came to know Lewis in his years at Magdalene I had so much guidance that I wish he could have been persuaded to write a piece for the book dealing with the Cambridge days; and finally, of course, I am grateful to all the others who so readily accepted my invitation to contribute chapters. I hope Lewis would have approved of this little book about him. He would certainly have had one or two things to say about its contents if not its concept. But he did tell me once 'After I have gone you can do what you like.' So at any rate I might be allowed to choose *my* ground this time; which I suppose he would say is what we have done with this book. He would surely forgive us.

J. G.

INTRODUCTION

BY

OWEN BARFIELD

W<small>HEN</small> I had finished devouring in typescript the seven chapters that follow, one of the things that most impressed me was the fact that Coghill's, which tells us most about himself, is also the one that tells us most about Lewis. I have taken the hint seriously . . . so seriously that I have closed for the occasion the anti-exhibitionism department of the censor's office, in order to put down some of the things that are uppermost in my mind about this most remarkable man.

Looking back over the last thirty years it appears to me that I have throughout all that time been thinking, pondering, wondering, puzzling over—not exactly the 'personality', but what I prefer to call the individual essence of my old friend. It will be understood that I have also had certain other matters to attend to—and yet to say *less* than that would somehow be an understatement. I first met him in 1919, and the puzzlement has had to do above all with the great change that took place in him between the years 1930 and 1940—a change which roughly coincided with his conversion to Theism and then to Christianity, but which did not appear, and does not appear in retrospect, to be inevitably or even naturally connected with it.

I remember very well the occasion on which I first became aware of it. I was staying at the Kilns, and Lewis had handed me either the typed or the already printed version of his *Open Letter to Tillyard*. It is now the third chapter of *The Personal Heresy*, but I am reminded by Mr Hooper's princely Bibliography that it was first printed separately in 1934, so that pretty well fixes the date. I remember reading it with the admiration and pleasure with which I read nearly everything Lewis wrote, whether in prose or verse; but also with a certain underlying—what is the word?—restlessness, *malaise*, bewilderment—that gradually increased until, when I came to the passage at the end:

> As I glance through the letter again I notice that I have not been able, in the heat of argument, to express as clearly or continuously as I could have wished my sense that I am engaged with 'an older and a better soldier'. But I have little fear that you will misunderstand me. We have both learnt our dialectic in the rough academic arena where knocks that would frighten the London literary coteries are given and taken in good part; and even where you may think me something too pert you will not suspect me of malice. If you honour me with a reply it will be in kind; and then, God defend the right!

> I am, my dear Sir, with the greatest respect,
> Your obedient servant,
>
> C. S. LEWIS.

I slapped down the book, or MS, and shouted: 'I don't believe it! It's *pastiche*!' I can't recall what comment he made (he may have been pouring out a drink or something) and, although I had shouted, I was not sure enough of my own judgment to press the point. It was a long time before I became clearly enough aware of what I meant to formulate it as I am doing now.

One other memory from a much later period; in the 50s, I think: Lewis would usually send me any poem he wrote and I always responded with some sort of comment. I cannot identify the particular poem I am now referring to, but on this occasion, after generally praising it, I added as an afterthought that it left me with the impression, not of an 'I say this', but of a 'This is the sort of thing a man might say'. Next time he wrote, he said this remark had raised an important question which we should have to discuss; he was not at all sure that the distinction could really be maintained. Incidentally I am not all that sure myself; and I do not recall that we ever in fact discussed it.

Perhaps these two recollections, taken together, sufficiently suggest the sort of thing I have pondered; and not less since his death than before it. *Was* there something, at least in his impressive, indeed splendid, literary personality, which was somehow—and with no taint of insincerity—*voulu*? So that, taken in conjunction with his immersion in the literature of the past and his imaginative power of vigorously re-animating it, there was something there that would justify my involuntary exclamation . . . some touch of a more than merely *ad hoc* pastiche?

From more than one observation in the chapters which follow it will appear that this was not the sort of question one could very well discuss with Lewis himself. I suspect it is one that raised issues he would have refused to contemplate. My close friendship with him did not however prevent me from continuing to puzzle and to ponder it; and, rightly or wrongly, I felt free to do so. As far as my own attitude is concerned, it seems to me that nothing could be less like impertinent curiosity and that my deep interest in him was, and is, one with my deep love for him.

As to what I mean by 'a more than merely *ad hoc* pastiche': Dr Farrer speaks here of Lewis's 'detachment from passing fashions' and adds later that 'he was never quite at home in what we may call our post-positivist era'. I remember, too, Alan Watts's (to my mind justified) comment in his book *Behold the Spirit:* 'a certain ill-concealed glee in adopting an old-fashioned and unpopular position. . . .'

But what I have in mind goes deeper than all this—so deep that it has long been inextricably entangled in my own mind with the whole problem of the relation between human feeling and human will ... with the very meaning of terms like, personality, persona, literary personality, spontaneity, sincerity, grace, talent, genius. The tangle pulls both ways. If I think of Lewis, I tend to start thinking of these things—or some of them —but neither can I think long of these things without his almost at once putting in an appearance in my reflections. And as, about the one, so about the other, I never succeed in arriving at any satisfactory conclusion.

I must add, I think, that I do not rule out the possibility of my being on the wrong track altogether; making it all needlessly complicated. Perhaps after all what I have been indulging in is no more than a common bit of over-elaborated psychologism *à la mode*, our twentieth-century rococo. On that view what happened around 1934 was, quite simply, that Lewis's genius came into its own, as it emerged for the first time from the husk of his previous immaturity. Anyone may take that view, and perhaps I should be rather relieved than distressed to have it conclusively demonstrated to me that he was right. In what I have said already, and in what follows, I am not advancing a thesis or making a case, but rather recording a piece of my own biography, because that *may* be judged relevant to a full understanding of CSL.

During the same period there were other external and circumstantial changes. For some years down to 1930 I had been living, in a village near Oxford, a life of occupational freedom, and we could meet and talk much more frequently than was ever afterwards possible. Moreover, when, at the end of that year, I entered the law and went to live in London, I had written and published two books which, in their limited sphere, could both be regarded as successes. He on the other hand had only *Spirits in Bondage* and *Dymer* to his credit and, if my puny sales were only in four figures, his were still in three. This remained the position until the *Pilgrim's Regress* appeared in 1935, after which he never looked back, but appeared to my dazzled eyes to go on for the rest of his life writing more and more successful books at shorter and shorter intervals.

These changes however only served to emphasize the changeless element in our friendship. As to his growing reputation and the fact that he was quickly becoming a well-known public figure—let me record for the sheer pleasure of it that throughout the whole of his life I never recall a single remark, a single word or silence, a single look, the lightest flicker of an eyelid or hemi-demi-semitone of alteration in the pitch of his voice, which would go to suggest that he felt his opinion entitled to more respect than that of old friends he was talking with because, unlike theirs, it had won the ear of tens or hundreds of thousands wherever the English language is spoken and in a good many places where it is not. I wonder how many famous men there have been of whom this could truthfully be said.

My move to London and into captivity meant only the substitution of a regular termly visit to Oxford for the older more casual and more frequent intercourse. It became by custom a long week-end, with Friday night in his rooms at Magdalen and Saturday afternoon and Sunday at the Kilns, in Headington Quarry, his private home. We no longer argued intensively, but in some ways this long stretch was the best of all in our friendship; and we continued, throughout, our earlier practice of reading together. We had finished the *Paradiso* before my move and we now went back to the *Inferno* and the *Purgatorio* and read also the *Iliad*, some Greek plays, most of the *Aeneid*, and much else; we were half-way through the *Odyssey* when the Second World War broke out. It was only the Second World War, moreover, that put an end to a custom dating back to the 20s—the annual spring walking-tour, in company with one or

more of the following: A. C. Harwood, W. E. Beckett (afterwards Sir Eric Beckett, Legal Adviser to the Foreign Office),
Leo Baker, Walter Field, Colonel Hanbury Sparrow, Professor
Tolkien, and (on one occasion) Lewis's former pupil, Griffiths
(afterwards Dom Bede Griffiths).

Thus, there was on the one hand a serene, unbroken continuity in our friendship and on the other, the two personal
changes (one of them being his 'conversion'), of which I have
spoken. This brought about a curious result. From about 1935
onwards (though here again it was only much later that I so
formulated it) I had the impression of living with, not one, but
two Lewises; and this was so as well when I was enjoying his
company as when I was absent from him. Mostly, of course, I
was absent. But either way there was both a friend and the
memory of a friend; sometimes they were close together and
nearly coalesced; sometimes they seemed very far apart. This
experience gradually became something like an obsession with
me, and it must have been somewhere about 1950 (when I was
still concerned to write verse) that I made it part of the emotional base for a long narrative poem. There were other things I
felt the need of unloading as well, and I ended by meditating at
some length, and ultimately writing, a sort of extension and
combination of two well-known Greek myths in such a way
that the characters and events should symbolize, at different
levels, a good many matters which I liked to think were still at
a 'pre-logical' stage in my mind . . . questions to which I did
not yet know the answers and knew that, for the purposes of
the poem, it was better that I should not know them.

Among the various themes, or experiences, which underlay
this effusion or were woven together in it, the thread that ran
most clearly through it all, which I rarely lost sight of altogether in the writing, and which most effectively determined
the structure of the whole *œuvre*, was the fact that two of the
characters loosely and archetypally represented for me 'my'

two Lewises. They suffered very different fates. The one (Perseus), after going through a great many difficulties arising out of a preference he had developed for dealing with the reflections of things rather than with the things themselves (the objective correlative here was an excessive use, for administrative purposes, of the mirror which had once enabled him to slay the Gorgon), made peace with what Professor Wilson Knight or Sir Herbert Read would probably call his 'creative eros' (Andromeda) and was ultimately constellated, along with Andromeda and Pegasus, in the heavens. The other (Bellerophon), after slaying the monster Chimera, declined an invitation to ascend to heaven on the back of Pegasus, who had been his mount in the fateful contest, on the ground of impiety. He was thrown by Pegasus and ended his days in increasing obscurity as a kind of aging, grumbling, earth-bound, guilt-oppressed *laudator temporis acti*.

These were the hard bones of the story—but of course there was a lot of incidental fun (especially with Pegasus), and I recall that I invented a new stanza for the job. In accordance with established custom I showed the poem to Lewis both while it was writing and after it was finished, but I said nothing at first of its personal connection with himself. A year or two later, however, I seized an occasion for disclosing this also, having some idea that my insight, if such it was, might just conceivably be of some service to him—and that this was the most delicate way of placing it at his disposal in case that should be so. I have already emphasized that it was not the sort of thing one could discuss *directly* with him. But now comes the main point of the anecdote. Five or six years later still (I think it would be) in some connection or other I pointed out to him that I had once written a long poem 'about' him. *He had completely forgotten!*

A simple and mildly comic explanation at once suggests itself. But it will not hold water. It was not the poem he had forgotten; not only had he thought well of it, but there never was a man like him for remembering his friends' verse, whether published or unpublished. He would quote, in middle or near-old age, a line from juvenilia dating back to the twenties, which they had long lost sight of themselves; I even found a line and half of my own in the last of the posthumous *Letters to Malcolm: Chiefly on Prayer*. What he *had* forgotten was the poem's avowed connection with himself.

If it is true that Lewis was not much interested in depth-psychology, it is not true that he had never thought about it. As a young man, for instance, he had been quite aware of the technique of diagnosing the psyche in terms of its latent perversion—and quite capable of applying this technique to himself, and incidentally to me. What I think is true is, that at a certain stage in his life he deliberately ceased to take any interest in himself except as a kind of spiritual alumnus taking his moral finals. I think this was part of the change to which I have referred; and I suggest that what began as deliberate choice became at length (as he had no doubt always intended it should) an ingrained and effortless habit of soul. Self-knowledge, for him, had come to mean recognition of his own weaknesses and shortcomings and nothing more. Anything beyond that he sharply suspected, both in himself and in others, as a symptom of spiritual megalomania. At best, there was so much else, in letters and in life, that he found much *more* interesting! As far as I am able to judge, it was this that lay behind that distinctive combination of an almost supreme intellectual and 'phantastic' maturity, laced with moral energy, on the one hand, with—I can find no other phrase for it—a certain psychic or spiritual immaturity on the other, which is detectable in some of his religious and theological writings; and occasionally elsewhere: for example, in the undergraduate humour of Weston and Devine's humiliation before Oyarsa in *Out of the Silent Planet* and the opera-bouffe climax of *That Hideous Strength* . . . is this Kathleen Raine's 'a kind of boyish greatness'? No doubt one is on dangerous ground here, where every word begs a question, and no doubt his definition of maturity and that of many of his followers would differ somewhat from my own. But, if I were arguing it with him personally, I should endeavour to short-circuit all that by putting forward as my example of spiritual maturity his own master, George Macdonald.

Thinking, feeling, and willing . . . the true relation between them . . . talent . . . genius . . . greatness . . . C. S. Lewis . . . where (I am always potentially asking myself) shall I find more light on them all? Only the other day the question again actualized itself as I was reading one of Coleridge's annotations to his copy of Southey's *Life of Wesley*:

> I am persuaded that Wesley never rose above the region of logic and strong volition. The moment an idea presents itself to him, his understanding intervenes to eclipse it, and he sub-stitutes a conception by some process of deduction. Nothing is *immediate* to him. Nor could it be otherwise with a mind so ambitious, so constitutionally—if not a commanding—yet a *ruling* genius; i.e. no genius at all, but a height of talent with unusual strength and activity of individual will.

This acute analysis of John Wesley's mental temper seems to me to have some bearing on Lewis's; though I wonder if the great drawer-of-the-line between fancy and imagination had not forgotten for a moment that there is more than one kind of genius—that there is a genius of the will (Napoleon, Loyola, Augustine) as well as of the imagination. One recalls, too, his own definition of genius in the chapter on Shakespeare's verse in the *Biographia Literaria* . . . 'possessing the spirit, not possessed by it'. In particular, knowing what the term *idea* signified to Coleridge, the two phrases 'an idea presents itself to him' and 'nothing is *immediate* to him' were resonant in me to the main issue between Lewis and myself during that period before the change, when the 'Great War', as he calls it in *Surprised by Joy*, was still going on between us. It is the issue that underlies the

B

four drawings (he could draw well and amusingly when he wanted to) included in a letter he sent me at that time, which were intended to illustrate our respective philosophical positions. They were labelled: *What you think you are doing; What I think you are doing; What you think I am doing; What I think I am doing.*

At that time the obsession had been, for a short space, the other way round. 'I am often surprised,' he had written me not long before, apologizing for some brusqueness in argument, which he had probably imagined—of which I certainly had not complained, 'at the extent to which your views occupy my mind when I am not with you and at the animosity I feel towards them.' And it was about the same time, or a little later, that he further expressed his own position in the form of a short story about a man born blind, who recovered his sight by an operation. The result was disastrous for the protagonist, because he insisted on trying to *see* the mysterious thing he had heard people calling 'light'; whereas you do not see light itself, but only the objects it illumines.[1]

Light is what you see *by*; it is not anything you see, or ever can or will see . . . for me, precisely this dilemma—of the light being in the world and the world 'knowing' it not, because it *is* within it—had become the very thing which the Baptist pointed to, and the overcoming of it, the very thing which Christ was born and died to bring about. For him it was S. W. Alexander's ineluctable contradiction between 'enjoyment' and 'contemplation' in *Space, Time and Deity*. Lewis was not yet a believing Christian, and even after he became one I was never sure how seriously he took the opening verses of St John's

---

[1] As far as I know, this was never published. He told me afterwards he had been informed by an expert that the acquisition of sight by a blind adult was not in fact the shattering experience he had imagined for the purposes of his story. Years later I found in one of Sir Julian Huxley's books an allusion to the initial results of such an operation, which suggested that Lewis had in fact imagined them pretty accurately.

Gospel. We argued it (as we argued most things that we argued at all) on his ground rather than mine—psychological, philosophical, aesthetic—with myself stammeringly, incoherently, and with his help, maintaining that the fundamental 'law of thought' (contradictories cannot both be true), in which he educated me and which I amused him by nicknaming 'Cox and Box', requires as its correlative, if it is not to reduce all thinking to sterility and ultimately to tautology or nonsense, the no less fundamental *imagination* of the polarity of contraries (Coleridge's 'polar logic'). Without the one, he pointed out, no communication ... 'we might as well give up talking altogether'! Without the other, I strugglingly groped towards replying, no expression, no meaning to communicate, no life. But I wish very much that I had been able to focus the difference between us as clearly then as I hope I am doing now.

'Barfield,' he wrote towards the end of his life in a letter to an American who was thinking of visiting this country, 'cannot talk on any subject without illuminating it'.[1] And I record this for two reasons. First, it underlies the enigmatic significance of my anecdote about the poem, since it indicates that he thought me less than a fool. If he had been even a tenth as much interested as, rightly or wrongly, most of us are in ourselves and the figure we cut, he could never have forgotten its connection with himself, as he did. Secondly, because it affords some justification for the attempt I have been making here to illuminate *one* subject, which has long been as full of interest to many others as it was insipid to himself. It is one particular beam from one particular source, and there may well be darkness in it as well. Nevertheless I thought I had better try.

If I have done nothing else, I must have succeeded in showing why I turned with so much interest and pleasure to the essays of

[1] I am indebted for this quotation to Professor Clyde S. Kilby, of Wheaton College, Illinois, author of *The Christian World of C. S. Lewis*. Wm. Eerdmans, Grand Rapids 1964.

which this book is composed. The reader will compare them for himself with what I have written, and it is well that he should do so. There is, for instance, the question I left open at the beginning: whether I have been making a great deal of psychological fuss about very little. I would think that Stella Gibbons's contribution, and possibly Dr Walsh's and Professor Bennett's might well suggest that I have; and certainly I have no wish to persuade anyone to the contrary. On the other hand some of the observations in Professor Coghill's and Professor Lawlor's essays—perhaps also in Dr Farrer's (I wonder by the way whether our era is quite so 'post-positivist' as he assumes) —may gain something in depth from what I have attempted to add.

It is an attempt I should never have made at all unless in that context and with that encouragement. For these other contributors give body to all I have left unsaid except in my casual reference to Lewis's 'almost supreme' maturity. They will emphasize for me that, in saying that, I meant exactly what I said and no less. It was not only Mr Lawlor, in his youth, who felt in his conversations with Lewis that he was wielding a pea-shooter against a howitzer. I have felt much the same all my life. Or was it more like trying to run along beside a motorcar in top gear? In other respects, too, I could confirm nearly all they say. I only have a very small quarrel here and there . . . with Professor Lawlor, for instance, for affirming that 'Lewis had not the least conception of Eliot's view that we need the past in order to understand the present', unless the words 'Eliot's view' are to be taken as so operative that the rest hardly count . . . and with Professor Bennett for describing *Till We Have Faces* as an 'allegory'. It is in my opinion the most muscular and powerful product of Lewis's imagination, as certainly as *The Abolition of Man* is his most powerful essay in discursive argument. It is much more a myth in its own right that it is an allegory: and if he had not previously written both a book about allegory and an avowed allegory of his own, it might have been properly appraised as such.

I am fairly often approached for general comment on C. S. Lewis or for an 'explanation' of his attitude to this or that. This used to be so even during his life. Such requests always make me feel both embarrassed and fraudulent. As if *I* could explain anything! He stood before me as a mystery as solidly as he stood besides me as a friend. It is mainly because of his not infrequent, and always generous, allusions to myself in his published writings that I have thought it well, while there is still time, to get all this written into the record—and with a maximum of candour.

I

The Christian Apologist

BY

AUSTIN FARRER

A Christian apologist, strictly speaking, is a writer who answers an attack. An advocate who takes the initiative is simply a preacher or an expositor. The first writing apologists for Christianity laboured to remove the misunderstandings or downright calumnies which justified the persecution of their faith. When pagans thought the Church worth writing against, apologetic took the shape of book answering book. So Origen replied to Celsus in form, though not, alas, with an answering brevity. Apology as such, then, is the refutation of a criticism; but it must be virtually impossible to write pure apology. You cannot well oppose the accusation of social disruptiveness without making a case for the cohesive tendencies of the gospel; you cannot clear the charge of silliness without establishing a claim to rationality. But the name of apology remains so long as hostile criticism provides the starting-point. A systematic theologian may vindicate the rationality of the faith more solidly than any apologist; but he does so simply by thinking it out and articulating the parts. He looks for the heart and sense of the doctrine. The apologist's eye is on the point of attack. He is a frontiersman.

There are frontiersmen and frontiersmen, of course. There

is what one might call the Munich school, who will always sell the pass in the belief that their position can be more happily defended from foothills to the rear. Such people are not commonly seen as apologists. They are reckoned to be New Theologians. They are too busy learning from their enemies to do much in defence of their friends. The typical apologist is a man whose every dyke is his last ditch. He will carry the war into the enemy's country; he will yield not an inch of his own.

Lewis was an apologist from temper, from conviction, and from modesty. From temper, for he loved an argument. From conviction, being traditionally orthodox. From modesty, because he laid no claim either to the learning which would have made him a theologian or to the grace which would have made him a spiritual guide. His writings certainly express a solid confidence; but it is the confidence that he can detect the fallacy of current objections to belief, and appreciate the superiority of orthodox tenets over rival positions; that he has some ability, besides, to make others see what he so clearly sees himself. These are modest claims, when compared with the pretension to look deeply into the things of God: a pretension he never advanced, even by implication, either on intellectual or on spiritual grounds.

The day in which apologetic flourishes is the day of orthodoxy in discredit; an age full of people talked out of a faith in which they were reared. To say that they want to believe if they could only see how is doubtless to simplify, for who are *they*? Which is the self, among all the warring selves in any breast? The very thing that reconversion does is to persuade a man to take a believing self as his fundamental self. We may say at the best that belief is a real (if smothered) attitude in such minds; and it is this that offers an opening to the apologetic approach. 'You have been rattled and browbeaten,' says the apologist. 'You have been sold a false image of faith and an inflated estimate of her enemies. Give faith her rights, and you will again believe.'—'Thank you, we will,' replies a grateful audience.

Educated England provided a field for Lewis's apologetic in the 'thirties and 'forties; America does so still. His present fame and influence in the United States will astonish his most enthusiastic English friends. But then America is a far less de-Christianized country than England. Where the erosion of orthodoxy has gone beyond a certain point, other champions and different arms are called for. There can be no question of offering defences for positions which are simply unoccupied, or of justifying ideas of which the sense has never dawned on the mind.

Lewis's characteristic attitude in his religious writings is that of an apologist, his procedures are not all equally apologetic; and it may well be that the less they are so the more effective they prove. The strictly apologetic technique is that of controversial argument; and it is no doubt essential to the apologist's success that he should enter the controversial lists with credit, and make a brave show in the exchange of buffets. Orthodoxy must be made out as argumentatively sound as any other position; but it may seldom be argument that casts the decisive weight. It may more commonly be a direct presentation, allowing the vitality of orthodox ideas to be felt.

The great value of Lewis as apologist was his many-sidedness. So far as the argumentative business went, he was a bonny fighter. His writing gave the same impression as his appearances in public debate. I was occasionally called upon to stop a gap in the earlier programmes of Lewis's Socratic Club. Lewis was president, but he was not bound to show up. I went in fear and trembling, certain to be caught out in debate and to let down the side. But there Lewis would be, snuffing the imminent battle and saying 'Aha!' at the sound of the trumpet. My anxieties rolled away. Whatever ineptitudes I might commit, he would maintain the cause; and nobody could put Lewis down.

It is commonly said that if rational argument is so seldom the cause of conviction, philosophical apologists must largely be wasting their shot. The premise is true, but the conclusion does not follow. For though argument does not create conviction, the lack of it destroys belief. What seems to be proved may not be embraced; but what no one shows the ability to defend is quickly abandoned. Rational argument does not create belief, but it maintains a climate in which belief may flourish. So the apologist who does nothing but defend may play a useful, though preparatory, part. Why, even Butler's *Analogy*, if we are to believe historical testimony, opened polished ears to the message of the Gospel. Yet no one can call the *Analogy* theophanic; there are no chinks in that unremitting continuity of prose through which celestial light shines.

Lewis did better. He provided a positive exhibition of the force of Christian ideas, morally, imaginatively, and rationally. The strength of his appeal (we have said) lies in the many-sidedness of his work. Christian theism, to those who believe it, commends itself as fact, not theory, by the sheer multiplicity of its bearings. Were it a speculation, it would surely face a single field of enquiry: it would assign the cause of the world, or the principle of duty, or the aim of existence, or the means of spiritual regeneration. If an equal light falls from a single source in all these directions at once, that source must seem to have the richness of a reality, rather than the abstract poverty of an idea. An admirable introduction to Lewis's religious work bears the title, *The Christian World of C. S. Lewis.*[1] No title could have been more happily chosen. The Lewis who has cleared the ground by his controversial argument admits his readers to a mental world of great richness, great vigour and clarity, and in every corner illuminated by his Christian belief.

[1] By Professor Clyde S. Kilby.

You cannot read Lewis and tell yourself that Christianity has no important moral bearings, that it gives no coherence to the whole picture of existence, that it offers no criteria for the decision of human choices, that it is no source of strength or delight, no effective object of loyalty.

In many different tones of voice we refer to the Middle Ages as ages of faith; a time in which men believed a heavenly Jerusalem above the sky much as they believed an earthly Sion beyond the sea; when the whole of their thought was of a piece with their theology. The picture is surely mythical, if it is set up as the picture of an entire Christendom. But we can say at least that those were days when a thoughtful soul here or there could realize some unity of mental vision. The fact should be admitted, however we regard it—whether as the stultifying tyranny of dogma or as an enviable single-mindedness: an ideal too easily realized, no doubt, in a plentiful dearth of empirical knowledge, and yet establishing a standard after which perplexed modernity may strive. We may read old authors, then, to see what it is to have a Christian mind. We need not, indeed, go back to the thirteenth century for our examples, the earlier seventeenth may serve; or (since there are disadvantages in going back at all) we can find what we want at home: we can step into a Christian world by opening Lewis.

Or will that be to go back nevertheless? Did not Lewis achieve a Christian mind by living in a prescientific world? To say so is the easiest way of writing him off as a thinker. Lewis lent a seeming support to the accusation in his inaugural lecture at Cambridge, by the ironical presentation of himself as the last survivor of an antediluvian species. But that was a trick of rhetoric. He had no interest on the occasion in assessing whether he were an antediluvian or not. What he desired was to gain a hearing for an exposition of medieval literature from a medieval point of view. 'Grant that you will be justified in writing me off as an antediluvian,' he says, 'but that will be a poor reason for refusing my testimony to the way things went before the Flood.' In a more serious mood he would denounce the heresy which placed expiry dates on moral or metaphysical opinions, as though they were tins of food, not fit for consumption more than a decade after they were canned. The attitude he wished to commend finds expression in his posthumous work, *The Discarded Image*. In that work, to the great advantage of students, he makes the late-Medieval world-view as clear and consistent as it would have been in Lewis's mind, had he lived then. Having exhibited its beauties, he detaches himself from it. It squared (more or less) with the empirical knowledge of its time; but it was no better than a myth. Those who have followed him through the exercise, he concludes, may not only understand the medievals better—they may be better placed for viewing with a reasonable detachment the scientific myths of their own age. Scientific formulae may be empirically verified, but no science-based picture of the sum of things is better than a symbol.

Whatever Lewis's mould of thought may have been, he did not (how could he?) believe in intellectual reaction. As he claimed the right to enjoy the literature of any period for the joy that was in it, so he claimed the liberty to profit from the insights of every generation open to his study. He would have been ashamed to know nothing of what was being said, written, or done in his own day; but he felt under no obligation to find it better than the products of previous time, and especially than those which had passed the sieve of old oblivion. No doubt if you are travelling up and down the ages, you have less leisure for chasing every hare put up by contemporary discussion. But then if you are really fascinated by the passing moment, you will never get beyond the newspapers.

It is surely senseless to set up standards of engagement with the present which are to be binding upon anyone we will consent to take seriously on any subject. It depends on what a writer is trying to do. Lewis in his religious writings was concerned to relate the changeable to the Changeless; and it was the Changeless rather than the changeable that needed to be brought into view. The special excellence of his apologetic was not undermined by his detachment from passing fashions; it was all of one piece with it. You cannot expect a writer whose peculiar merit is a massive entirety of view to play chameleon to every passing colour of conflicting doctrine. A contrasted example will bring out the point. Lewis lived just long enough to comment somewhat unsympathetically on Dr John Robinson's excursion into the field of popular theology. It was not to be expected that he should care for it; for what could be less congenial to his mind? The Bishop of Woolwich captures the attention of his readers by showing them that he is as intellectually worried, as dissatisfied with orthodoxy, and as unable to reconcile conflicting insights as they are themselves. They are consoled to think that there is not that iron curtain between the official Church and the contemporary mind which they had supposed; they are free to hope that Christian faith can be had on tolerable terms and without achieving any strict coherence of ideas. Lewis's appeal was just the opposite. Muddled minds read him, and found themselves moving with delight in a world of clarity.

What are we to say of the two approaches? Perhaps they are adapted to different men, or to different times. But supposing that either is equally practicable, there is no question which takes us further. The one opens the hope of thinking towards belief, the other supplies an exercise in believing thought. It is not, of course, fair to make a direct comparison between men so differently placed: Lewis's approach is not open to Robinson. A lay professor and one-time atheist can say to the world, 'Look and see that such a man as I am can be an orthodox Christian.' What can a prelate say?

'Look and see that a struggling enquirer can be a suffragan bishop.'

Either approach may have its place. The criticism (anyhow) which disallows Lewis's on principle must be set aside as a begging of the question. A voice which says 'You must adopt the posture of an admittedly de-Christianized world; you may wriggle into a Christian attitude if you can' is presuming that neither the authority of revelation nor the doctrine of original sin can be taken seriously. It sounds well to say that the true prophet is a revolutionary, going further and faster than the forward movement of the age; but the dictum bears little relation to experience. The prophets have resisted the current of their times; and they have found a footing for their stand in whatever firm ground past history seemed to afford them. It would require a more than common effrontery of paradox, to present Jeremiah as the nose on the face of the Zeitgeist.

The champion of a perennial faith must admittedly speak to his contemporaries' condition, and establish an effective dialogue with them. It is no use proving on *a priori* grounds that Lewis failed to do these things, when his success over the whole English-speaking world shows the contrary. Of course that world is not of one piece. No author writes for the two hundred million. Lewis was able to reach a surprisingly wide stratum of the better educated. Or by an effective dialogue with the age, do you mean an effective dispute with its most admired philosophers? But to take up the cudgels at philosophical congresses or in the pages of *Mind* is a business to occupy a professional. Philosophy was not Lewis's trade and he had many other irons in the fire. He was singularly successful in so far challenging philosophical influences current during the thirties as to make a place for Christian belief in the minds of university students, and some of them by no means the least intelligent. He was never quite at home in what we may call our post-positivist era; his philosophical commendations of

theism cannot usefully be recommended to puzzled undergraduate philosophers of the present day. His literary, his
moral, and his spiritual development was continuous; his
philosophical experience belonged to the time of his conversion. Philosophy is an ever-shifting, never-ending public discussion, and a man who drops out of the game drops out of
philosophy. But theological belief is not a philosophical position, it is the exercise of a relation with the most solidly real of
all beings; and there are many lights in which it may be
placed other than those of philosophical discussion. It does not
follow that a Christian apologist who drops out of professional
philosophy is left with nothing to say.

So far I have written somewhat at large about the apologetic
effect of Lewis's religious writings. Many of them are not for-
mally apologetic. *Screwtape* and *The Great Divorce* are not
written to repel attacks or to resolve difficulties; nor are the
talks collected in *Mere Christianity*. Here we have plain exposi-
tions or imaginative realizations of doctrine; above all, moral
analysis displaying the force of Christian ideas. The autobio-
graphical pieces—*Pilgrim's Regress* and *Surprised by Joy*—con-
tain the intellectual history of conversion rather than straight
apology. Apart from short essays and occasional papers,
Miracles and *The Problem of Pain* are the most direct examples
of Lewis's apologetic writing. The subjects of these two books,
indeed, make them apologetic in a double sense. For they deal
with apparent stumbling-blocks to faith, which may rouse
anxious questions in believing hearts, quite apart from the
cavils of sceptics on the special impact of new knowledge.
There appears to be at these points an intrinsic need for justifying the ways of God to men.

Let us then take *The Problem of Pain* as an example of Lewis's
apologetic qualities. '*The Problem of Pain*? Surely not. How can
we take *The Problem of Pain* seriously now that we have *A Grief
Observed*? When his wife died, Lewis felt the reality about

which he had so airily theorized and his theories were of no consolation or assistance in the hour of trial. He had to find the existential solution.' He did indeed; and when he had found it, what reason had he either to repudiate or alter anything he had written in *The Problem of Pain*? When he wrote the earlier book, he did not imagine that the sting of agony could be drawn by speculation. But speculation has its place. Those who wish to be spared the trouble of thought are happy to quote the reported saying from the last days of St Thomas Aquinas; something had just been spiritually revealed to him which made everything he had written look like old rope. Yet the value of St Thomas to Christendom does not lie in that single remark; it lies in the order he was able to establish among our theological ideas. If a man is groping after some apprehension of transcendant deity, it is not useful to tell him that always supposing he lives a devoted life, he may hope, towards the end of it, for a revelation such as St Thomas received (though, on statistical evidence, he has a very slight percentage chance of getting it). Nor is it much good to tell a man labouring to conceive the Providence of God in spite of the evils rampant in his Creation, that if after prolonged bachelordom he makes a blissful marriage and loses his wife in a couple of years by an agonizing disease, he will then (should his faith survive) have reason to tell himself that nothing further of the sort is likely to shake it.

If Lewis had not written *The Problem of Pain* already, he might have written it, with no doubt some difference of emphases, after he recovered from the blow recorded in *A Grief Observed*. Indeed, when he wrote *The Problem*, he already had plenty of experimental evidence. His recollections of early life show his feelings to have been alarmingly vulnerable. He had endured the First World War on the Western Front, and been severely wounded. And he had causes of personal grief, some disclosed in his writings, others only hinted at. He who has stood fire may fairly reflect on mortal combat; not, however, while he is dodging the bullets. Some people have no use for reflection; but that's another matter.

The first thing to strike us about *The Problem of Pain* is the modesty of its scale. It is a little book, not much more than 40,000 words; and it ranges over a wide area of topics. Its author can never have imagined that he would make a profound contribution to philosophical theology at this rate; and so we have the more reason to accept at their face value his introductory disclaimers. The book, he says, contains nothing original apart from marginal speculations in the last chapters on topics which Revelation leaves undefined. Elsewhere he believes himself to be restating old orthodox doctrines.

He could not well show himself more content to be unoriginal than he does in his first chapter. It is remarkable, indeed, that he should write such a chapter at all. Any academically-minded author attempting Lewis's subject would surely say, 'I am writing about the problem which the fact of pain presents to a Christian belief in God. Heaven knows the subject is wide enough. I cannot undertake here the previous question, why we should believe in God at all. If I handled the question seriously, it would take a book to itself; while to treat it perfunctorily would be to invite contempt.' But Lewis's aim is apologetic, and therefore pastoral. He knew his readers. They wrote to him from all over the world; he answered them in unbelievable number and with unfailing generosity. The author of *The Problem of Pain* realizes that the reader who picks up his book may never have read a serious discussion of theology before, and may never read another. Though such a reader approaches the subject through a concern over the problem of suffering, and not over the general issue of belief, he will find himself carried to a level of reflection at which he will inevitably ask, 'On what grounds after all does my inherited or instinctive faith in God rest?' It is characteristic of Lewis that

C

without reserve or affectation he does what he can. On the scale of a pamphlet in a church porch, he is prepared to handle the origins of theism. He takes the approach most likely to commend itself to an interest awakened by the problem of pain. The apparent distribution of goods and evils, of purpose and purposelessness (he says) makes it absurd to argue from the world to a Supreme Goodness. Were such the grounds of belief, the fact of pain (in the widest sense) might well cut them away. But, historically speaking, it is evident that religion springs from no such grounds. Lewis proceeds to give his textbook sketch of the development of religion. It contains no reference to his own evolution into belief; the special themes of *The Pilgrim's Regress* and *Surprised by Joy* are absent. He gives what he regards as the standard answer of the time—Biblical Revelation read through Rudolf Otto's spectacles: a world haunted by the supernatural, a conscience haunted by the moral absolute, a history haunted by the divine claim of Christ; such have been the accumulating strata of religious evidence.

Lewis is obliged to put his points so briefly as to be open to every attack. But the protection which his arguments lack in particular is made up to them in general. He concedes that the evidence of religion is not logically compulsive; and compensates for the admission by appealing to the fact that it has so widely prevailed with reasonable men. The chapter, slight as it is, provides an excellent example of the author's good management. Determined as he is to indicate the live sources of belief, he takes the necessary risks; yet he contrives to cover himself from the suspicion of fanaticism or of naïvety. And that without overloading his page, or saying more than can agreeably be said. So he gives to textbook matter the freshness of a living reconsideration.

When he turns to the substantial part of his essay, pastoral concern continues to rule his pen. Anyone who attempts that difficult theme will soon realize that a choice lies before him.

Is he to throw the weight on the philosophical or on the theological side? Philosophy can be called upon to show that the pains against which our hearts revolt are inseparable from sentient life in the only setting we can conceive for it. The argument has nothing directly to do with faith in God. It carries the corollary that if we do believe in God, we cannot fairly complain of his having made our world such as it is; for we cannot really conceive it radically different. So God's goodness is placed beyond attack, but at some risk of emptying out its practical significance. By calling the Creator good, we mean more, surely, than that it's no bad thing there should be a creation.

The theological approach boldly accepts belief in particular providence and seeks a setting for the incidence of pains in God's dealing with his human creatures. The advantage of the approach is its direct relevance to religion. A reader who is concerned to see pain and theism reconciled is presumably concerned with God and with a positive acceptance of his will; and an answer which relates our joys and sorrows to that will direct is more relevant than an answer which gives them the general support of a purpose underlying the world-order. The disadvantage of the theological approach is that, pressed to its logical extreme, it yields revolting paradoxes. If pain is the direct instrument of divine purpose, the divine hand is made responsible for afflictions which can have no other effect than the destruction of human personality. For this and other like reasons no one who knows what he is about can rely on the theological approach alone. We are bound to allow that the very nature of the physical world carries with it the chance of random and disastrous accident, however far we press the over-ruling of evils for providential ends.

But if the apologist is to use both approaches, the nicest point in his argument will be the relation between them. The nicest point—for academic minds; Lewis wastes no time upon it. His method of bracketing the two is purely verbal and expository. The problem of pain appears to arise from the definition of deity as an omnipotent goodness. Lewis takes the two defining terms one by one. To call God omnipotent, he says, is not to suppose he might do what would make no sense; for example, so to intervene in the natural field for the prevention of harms, as to stop nature's functioning naturally. Lewis closes the chapter, and gives 'good' its turn. God's goodness will not mean a spoiling indulgence; his aim need not be our ease so much as our perfection. The discussions of the two attributes seem to lie in the same plane. In fact they do not. The first expresses the philosophical approach, the second the theological. The light Lewis casts on omnipotence derives from the intrinsic character of the world's structure; the light he casts on goodness, from a consideration of the highest personal benevolence. How are the two discussions related to one another? If the requirements of world-structure are so inexorable, what scope is there for a free providence in distributing pleasures or pains? If pains are the natural rubs of a world-structure bearing on sentient creatures, what need have we to view them as instruments of a disciplinary providence?

The readers Lewis has in mind will not ask such questions. Having agreed that the world could not have been what it essentially is without a considerable incidence of pain, they will be ready to consider how God will govern such a world, and what divine purpose will be served by the way in which our pains affect us. It is this line of enquiry, anyhow, that Lewis follows out in the rest of his book. The philosophical approach falls into the background.

Towards the end of the chapter on divine goodness something happens to Lewis and something happens to his readers. His writing hitherto has been argumentative, clear, sympathetic, persuasive. Now it becomes something more. It is where he has taken up the objection that the disciplinary providence of the biblical religion is a jealous lover, whereas we have now learnt to detest possessiveness in love. In answering the objection he discloses the unique transcendent claim of the love of God with a controlled and reasonable passion which is theophanic. 'Yes,' says the willing reader, 'that is God.' We think we are listening to an argument, in fact we are presented with a vision; and it is the vision that carries conviction.

Lewis's next move is to justify from the condition of the patient a divine handling of which surgery is no less typical than are caresses. Are we really as sick as that? Lewis's chapter on human wickedness remains true to the form of apologetic argument, refuting one by one the convenient and fashionable doctrines which let us off moral self-examination. But in removing our defences he makes to us a terrible disclosure of ourselves and more particularly of our current attitude to ourselves. I do not see how it could be done with greater modesty or greater penetration. And so (says the reader) this is I.

Lewis's purpose is not to justify retribution (though he keeps a corner for it). It is to justify discipline or 'mortification' as a divine means for sanctifying us. The theme is pursued in a discussion of the Fall. The dogma of original sin, says Lewis, does not explain how the world can have been created good in spite of all its current flaws; nor yet does it justify the scourging of the present generation by saddling it with ancestral guilt. It simply records the part played by a misuse of free will in bringing our present predicament about. By so doing, the doctrine shows the appropriateness of a divine remedy addressed to the will; for it is on the will that mental pain comes to bear. What will has caused, will must be brought to correct.

In expounding the traditional opinion that racial or Adamic sin lies essentially in egotism or pride, Lewis has another of his terrible and searching passages. It is commonly said (and how reasonable it sounds) that you cannot argue from sin to holiness; until the appropriateness of submission to God has been acknowledged, what harm can be seen in human autonomy? If I have no other God, how can I help being God to myself? No position could sound more logical; and yet (as Lewis's passage shows) the claims for divine will can be felt in an exposure of self-will. In recognizing the deformity of pride we find ourselves perceiving the attraction of faith.

It is only after five chapters of preparatory matter that Lewis feels able to take up his professed topic, human pain. After what has gone before, it is evident that his concern will be to exhibit suffering as appropriate to our fallen condition. He briefly recurs to his 'philosophical' chapter, to remind us that the very constitution of the world opens the possibility of pain. Our own perversity has seized upon it; we have tormented one another, we have poisoned ourselves. Nevertheless, God's 'permission' of evil so multiplied is not simply to be accounted for by his respecting our free will. He takes the harms we mutually inflict and overrules them for our good.

The primary function of mental pain, says Lewis, is to force our misdirectedness on our attention. But just as it belongs to our fallen state to be blind to holiness until we suffer the consequence of sin, and blind to a higher good until natural satisfactions are snatched from us; so equally it belongs to our state that we cannot achieve disinterestedness until it costs us pain. Sympathy is made real by the sharing of distress, and martyrdom is the typical expression of devotion to God.

Such is the central answer Lewis gives to the problem he has undertaken to discuss; and it is difficult to deny that it is the distinctively Christian answer. Many other wise things can be said about the endurance of pain, but it is less evident that they arise out of the Christian revelation. Lewis allows his answer its full effect by disencumbering it of secondary apologetic points. He sweeps a collection of such points into a sort of appendix, and dumps them in a separate chapter.

We have now glanced at what it seems fair to call the most

solid part of the book. Lewis's argument achieves an astonishing power when he is able to commend basic orthodoxy to our moral perception. The whole argument is, in effect, a moral argument. He nowhere claims that the tribulations befalling mankind have on balance an improving effect. The utilitarian or statistical approach is foreign to his mind. He argues that our pains are a proper medicine. Whether we are willing to swallow it is another matter; discipline is addressed to the will and the will is free.

The corollary is hell for the impenitent, a conclusion which Lewis finds as inescapable as it is appalling. He calls on us to agree that if ultimate impenitence is possible, it is better it should feel the pain of truth; yes, even though it cannot see the truth to be true. Who can seriously approve an everlasting moral morphia for the refusers of heaven? So far the argument commends our grave respect. Lewis's further speculations on the state of the damned appear inconsistent and not altogether intelligible. How is one to compromise between an existence suffering the pain of truth, and such a dissolution of the mental being as might leave us sensitive to flame perhaps, but scarcely to remorse? Here if anywhere Lewis seems to forget for whom he is writing. No broad apologetic purpose can be achieved by such tortured speculations.

If the divine hand prefers our ultimate good to our present ease, we cannot well accept the dispensation unless we set our hopes on heaven. Lewis writes nobly about the final state; but before he ventures to do so he asks with commendable realism whether anyone hopes for heaven at all, or ever desires it. We may admire the diffidence with which he introduces in reply the darling theme of others among his writings— that romantic yearning after a transcendent joy, which he felt to have played so great a part in his own emotional and religious life. Do we, he now asks, ever fully desire anything *but* heaven, in whatever false guises we may look to find it? His diffidence in introducing the point appears to be twofold. He cannot tell how widely the experience to which he appeals will be recognized; and he does not feel sure of his theology. Is romantic yearning an appetite for heaven, or is it the ultimate refinement of covetousness? One cannot but respect his sense of responsibility in voicing his doubt about what so deeply moved him.

So far we may go in illustrating the force and excellence of Lewis's apologetic theology. If there were no more to be said, he would have had none but admirers, anyhow among minds sympathetic to belief. But he had foibles as well, which however secondary a part they play in his work, have been sufficient to cause irritation and estrangement. *The Problem of Pain* will also illustrate them.

First, then, the moralism which is the strength of his thought runs into excess and overbalances it. When I say moralism I do not mean legalism, an ethic of rules rather than of love. Lewis was a Christian, he was no pharisee. But when he considered man in relation to God he viewed him too narrowly as a moral will, and that relation too narrowly as a moral relation. Man, to Lewis, is an immortal subject; pains are his moral remedies, salutary disciplines, willing sacrifices, playing their part in a drama of interchange between God and him. But this is not all the truth, nor perhaps half of it. Pain is the sting of death, the foretaste and ultimately the experience of sheer destruction. Pain cannot be related to the will of God as an evil wholly turned into a moral instrument. Pain is the bitter savour of that mortality out of which it is the unimaginable mercy of God to rescue us. When under suffering we see good men go to pieces we do not witness the failure of a moral discipline to take effect; we witness the advance of death where death comes by inches. By failing to keep so elementary a consideration sufficiently in the forefront of his scene, Lewis risks forfeiting the sympathy of a compassionate reader, for all the evidences of a compassionate heart he abundantly displays.

Lewis was raised in the tradition of an idealist philosophy which hoped to establish the reality of the mental subject independently of, or anyhow in priority to, that of the bodily world. Though he moved some way from such positions he was still able to overlook the full involvement of the reasonable soul in a random and perishable system. Even when, in his second chapter, he is at pains to assert the inescapableness of the physical, he begins by taking spiritual persons as given quantities, that he may show how necessary to their activity and to their mental intercourse is the bodily medium in which they swim. It is a medium which has its inevitable clumsiness and which opens the possibility not merely of collision between persons, but of mutual attack. Only, of course, rational beings need not hurt one another except by involuntary accident. If they do so on purpose, it is culpable malice. When rational consciousness descends from heaven to meet and animate the evolving human creature, it does not (in Lewis's belief) find itself committed to the cause of a sentient body fighting all comers for dear life. Vegetables, he says, are mutually destructive by nature; animals are not; their present condition is a fallen condition.

At this point he involves himself in impossible difficulties. What he needs to say is that animal nature was still innocent when reason dawned on our part of it, and that only afterwards it shared the fall of man. But scientific evidence convinces him that carnivorous beasts were up to their tricks aeons before man had a free will to misuse. So he is driven to favour the speculation of a fall preceding that of Adam; some spiritual prince of this globe fell, and corrupted the animals long before man offered him an opportunity for moral seduction. Even then the sum won't add up—if the animals were fallen already, it was as a fallen animal that man acquired the first rudiments of reason, and so his initial innocuousness was after all a sudden miracle.

It would be possible to follow further the ramifications of this theme into speculations on the immortality of brutes; but I forebear. Lewis, we began by saying, was overbalanced on the side of moralism. But moralism of itself would not have carried him so far as this. Imagination has slipped from the leash of reason—even if it is a traditionalist imagination. His readers rub their eyes, and wonder what they are seeing— Lewis wrote fairy tales but surely he did not believe them! It adds to our stupefaction, rather than detracting from it, when he solemnly submits such fantasies to the censure of the Church. It is aberrations of this kind, rather than merited attacks on materialist philosophy, which fix on Lewis the label 'antiscientific'. What a pity it is that by such superfluous un-realities he should furnish the public with excuses to evade the overwhelming realism of his moral theology!

But there is nothing we can tell Lewis about himself that he did not know. The evidence is in his poems. Reason, he says, is the virginal Athena, Imagination is the fertile Demeter, and both deities must be duly honoured. But then he proceeds

> Oh who will reconcile in me both maid and mother,
> Who make in me a concord of the depth and height?
> Who make imagination's dim exploring touch
> Ever report the same as intellectual sight?
> Then could I truly say, and not deceive,
> Then wholly say, that I BELIEVE.

And last, since we have taken up his poems, we cannot con-clude without that pastiche of John Donne, in which Lewis reveals his deep sense of an Apologist's temptations.

> From all my lame defeats and oh! much more
> From all the victories that I seemed to score;

From cleverness shot forth on Thy behalf
At which, while angels weep, the audience laugh;
From all my proofs of Thy divinity,
Thou, who wouldst give no sign, deliver me.

Thoughts are but coins. Let me not trust, instead
Of Thee, their thin-worn image of Thy head.
From all my thoughts, even from my thoughts of Thee,
O thou fair Silence, fall, and set me free.
Lord of the narrow gate and the needle's eye,
Take from me all my trumpery lest I die.

2

'Grete Clerk'

BY

J. A. W. BENNETT

In a peroration that has become famous C.S.L. presented himself as one of the last representatives of the 'Old Western Order'.[1] The stance of a last survivor always attracted him; it is one of the likings that he shared with William Morris, and it early drew him to the sagas and the doomed Eddaic gods. It comes easily, perhaps too easily, to a traditionalist, especially to one who rejects the view that civilization is bound to increase, easily also to a Christian foreseeing a time when faith shall not be found on the earth. But Lewis also shared with Morris a sense that such thoughts should be put by: 'the answer is simply to get on with the job—to mend the sails, or launch the boat, or gather firewood'. And there is a danger that the mere quotability of his Cambridge Inaugural may lead us to forget his positive achievement in making the traditional culture that he loved attractive and accessible to new generations. Fine scholar though he was, he was an even

---

[1] *De Descriptione Temporum.* An Inaugural Lecture by the Professor of Medieval and Renaissance English Literature in the University of Cambridge, Cambridge University Press, 1955. Some passages in the present essay are reproduced from his successor's Inaugural Lecture, *The Humane Medievalist*, Cambridge University Press, 1965.

better teacher; and it may truly be said of him, as Newman said of Scott, that in turning men's minds to the Middle Ages he 'stimulated their mental thirst ... silently indoctrinating them with nobler ideas, which might afterwards be appealed to as first principles'.

Lewis's own regard for Scott (with whom he shared a liking for monarchy, and dogs) rested on grounds rather broader than Newman's—on the poignant and revealing Journals as much as on the novels. But my immediate point is that Newman's words about Scott many of us could apply to the author of *The Allegory of Love* and *The Discarded Image*. Admittedly the influence of a remote don—especially of a don who in unpropitious times dared *defend* his Chesterton—cannot be compared with a great novelist's, even allowing for Lewis's unique blend of imaginative and expository gifts. Yet it may fairly be urged that for multitudes who find Scott unreadable Lewis was the first to reveal the fascination of the Middle Age and, what is much more, to reveal its 'grande clarté'. It is true that in the early years of this century a similar office had been performed by several other writers; French, Scottish, and American. But to medieval studies in this country Lewis's logical and philosophical cast of mind gave a wholly new dimension. This can be concisely demonstrated by tracing throughout his works his concern with the philosophic and semantic developments of the terms *Phusis*, *Natura*, and *Kind*. They are the threads that led him to the door of the school of Chartres and through the garden of the Rose. He followed them in Chaucer, Spenser, even (when observing the rise of the Picturesque) in Addison; they provided the samples for the first and longest chapter of *Studies in Words*: a work that illustrates his learning at its ripest, his style at its easiest (so he would talk in an Oxford Common Room or a Cambridge Parlour)—and his prejudices at their frankest.

The chapter on the *Roman de la Rose* is the heart of *The*

Allegory of Love, and scholars from Texas to Montreal have in different ways justified his view of that gargantuan poem, with only Princeton recently raising a dissenting voice. But his book might equally well have been called *The Love of Allegory*; and one of its effects to make allegory both readable and respectable again. G. M. Young spoke for many 'lewed folke' when he said: 'it makes one feel what one imagines a tired and thirsty tree to feel under the rain'. I am not sure that Lewis's distinction between allegory and symbol can always be maintained—just as I am not sure that he has correctly stated the scholastic views on 'romantic' love—but I am sure that his later pages on allegory take us to the heart of medieval literature. Lewis was certainly not the first, nor the last, to be attracted by the school of Chartres. But in tracing its influence on the allegorists he took a special pleasure. The value he set on that school's assertion of the wholeness of man's nature is one reason for describing him as a humane medievalist.

Nature, Love, and Allegory (though not, or not much, medieval allegory) are such essential components of *The Faerie Queene* that Lewis could hardly have omitted Spenser from his book even had he wished. In fact his closing chapter was to be the first of three pleas for a reconsideration of Spenser, each with its own grace and cogency. It suggested that if any critic could set out all the shifts and strains of the sixteenth century it was he. And the Clark Lectures, in their original and still more in their expanded form as a volume in the *Oxford History of English Literature* left no doubt. Here at last was an Attendant Spirit to liberate us from the spells of Burkhardt or Addington Symonds and challenge the easy antithesis of fantastic and fideistic Middle Ages versus logical and free-thinking Renaissance. And it is a prime justification of medieval studies that if properly pursued they soon dispose of such facile distinctions, and overthrow the barriers of narrow specialism and textbook chronology. In this sense medieval just as much as classical studies make men more humane. It would indeed be hard to separate in Lewis's culture the one from the other: just as hard as it is to understand the Middle Ages themselves without knowing classical literature or the Renaissance without knowing the Middle Ages. This continuity of literature and of learning Lewis not only asserted but embodied. And in the last two years alone half a dozen specialist studies have quietly vindicated his approach to the Renaissance, and the justness of his criticisms of those arch-humanists who dismissed scholastic logic and philosophy as barbarous.

At this point it is salutary to remember that, bookish as he was (as bookish as his favourite medieval authors), his was not a purely literary culture. Not that he despised the tools of the literary trade. The first lectures of his that some of us attended were on textual criticism. To the study of metre he brought the fruits of lifelong experimentation in verse. And a certain clause in the Cambridge Ordinances did not inhibit him from the Study of Words in a way which was not precisely Archbishop Trench's nor yet Pearsall Smith's nor Professor Empson's, though it combined the virtues of all three. But what was chiefly novel in his equipment was the philosophical mind, sharpened in the fires of 'Greats'. And several pages in 'O.H.E.L.'—to resort to his favourite abbreviation—for his volume in the *Oxford History*—remind us that for many years he taught political theory, and so knew his Hobbes as well as his Hooker, his Machiavelli as well as his More. This unique combination of different kinds of learning did place him at a distance from his juniors, though one thought of him as a Johnsonian Colossus rather than a dinosaur. And here a passage on Johnson's style that he was fond of quoting from Ruskin's *Præterita* comes irresistibly to mind: that in which Ruskin praises ('because they were just, and clear') 'those sentences intended, either with swordsman's or paviour's blow to cleave an enemy's crest or drive down the oaken pile of a principle.'

Yet these images hardly convey the full impact of his lithe and lively mind or his pleasure in 'animated relaxation': at one moment challenging a pupil who had incautiously sneered at *Sohrab and Rustum*, at another analysing the preciosities of Amanda Mcitrick Ross's *Irene Iddesleigh* or *Poems of Puncture* (to read from these choice works of one of his father's clients was a long-standing test of sobriety at Magdalen 'Schools' dinners)—at another (later in the evening) composing, and enacting, a libretto for a mimic opera. Music (and not only Wagnerian music) provided him with some of his keenest pleasures: which may explain the particular delight he took in the medieval world-image with

> every planet in his proper sphere
> In moving makand harmony and sound.

Though he avoided the danger of conceiving that model to be completely Christian—he was too well read in Aristotle for that—he remained enthralled by the sublimely ordered Ptolemaic cosmos in which 'we do not see, like Meredith's Lucifer, the army of unalterable law but rather the revelry of insatiable love'. He conceded that it was not 'true'; but in his last, perhaps his most provocative, pages, claimed that all 'models' of the universe reflect as much the psychology of an age as the current state of knowledge.

In so far as he did not pursue scholarship as an end in itself (though he had a greater relish for it than most modern critics) he may seem inaccurately described as a humanist, especially as that term may nowadays likewise connote rationalist or epicurean or genteel dilettante. But *litterae humaniores* were his foundation, and they did in every sense make him more humane, enlarging his responses not restricting them. The whole man was in all his judgments and activities, and a discriminating zest for life, for 'common life', informs every page he wrote. He saw education as actualizing the potentiality for the leisured activities of thought, art, literature and conversation. 'Grete clerk' as he was, he was never wilfully esoteric: quotations and allusions rose unbidden to the surface of his full and fertile mind, but whether drawn from *Tristram Shandy* or James Thurber they elucidate not decorate. His works are all of a piece: a book in one genre will correct, illumine, or amplify what is latent in another. Hence the opening chapters of the *Allegory* must now be read in the light of the closing pages of *The Four Loves*—where he retracts his view that passionate love was largely a literary phenomenon; while those same pages lead us straight to the first theme of *The Discarded Image*—namely the appearance of pagan or neoplatonic elements in the formative writers of the medieval Christian tradition. The germ of *An Experiment in Criticism* is to be found in a paper on 'High and Low Brows' written some twenty-five years earlier. The Merlin who in a very literal sense underlies the action of *That Hideous Strength* is the Merlin who was to figure in his selections from Laȝamon's *Brut*. And in *Till We Have Faces* the expositor of allegory himself writes an allegory so haunting and so suggestive that it makes Fulgentius's allegorical interpretation of this tale of Cupid and Psyche seem strained, and Boccaccio's gloss on it merely mechanical.

Perhaps it is no accident that in describing the various writers of his idolatry he more than once lets fall a phrase that could equally apply to himself. 'To read Spenser,' he says, 'is to grow in mental health.' What he values in Addison is his 'open-mindedness'. The moments of despair chronicled in Scott's diary cannot, he claims, counterpoise 'that ease and good temper, that fine masculine cheerfulness' suffused through the best of the Waverley novels. Most of all it was the *chiaroscuro* of what Chaucer called 'earnest' and 'game' that attracted him. He found it eminently in the poetry of Dunbar that late-medieval Scottish maker who wrote the greatest religious

D

poetry and the earthiest satire in the language; and a favourite couplet of Dunbar's sums up his view of the whole duty and delight of Man:

> Man, please thy Maker and be merry
> And give not for this world a cherry.

3

The Approach to English

BY

NEVILL COGHILL

LEWIS AND I were both members of a discussion-class brilliantly presided over by Professor George Gordon in the Michaelmas Term of 1922, and that, I think, was how we first met. The class read papers to itself every week and presently it was Lewis's turn. He chose for his subject *The Faerie Queene* and I remember wondering what he could find to say of so vast a subject in so short a time as the hour of discussion allowed him, and whether it would be anything new. It will hardly count for new now, more than forty years later, but it seemed new then; repudiating the Hazlitt view that if you leave the allegory alone it will not bite you, he gave an account of the Spenserian world that championed its ethical attitudes as well as their fairy-tale terms, with a rich joy in the defeat of dragons, giants, sorcerers, and sorceresses by the forces of virtue; it was a world he could inhabit and believe in as one inhabits and believes a dream of one's own; its knights, dwarfs, and ladies were real to him, and became real even to me while he discussed them: he rejoiced as much in the ugliness of the giants and in the beauty of the ladies as in their spiritual significances, but most of all in the ambience of the faerie forest and plain that, he said, were carpeted with a grass greener than the common stuff of ordinary glades; this was the *reality* of grass, only to be apprehended in poetry: the world of the imagination was nearer to the truth than the world of the senses, notwithstanding its palpable fictions, and Spenser had transcended sensuality by making use of it, giving us the very sheen of grass—no! (he corrected himself), *sheen* was too feeble a word; he needed the Greek word γάνος to express the radiance of the reality of the greenness of Spenser's groves and glades, lawns, hills, and forests. It was like the Platonic idea of greenness, a spiritual reality. Lewis seemed to carry the class with him in his combative pleasure; his paper made a strong effect. It was certainly the best the class had heard, and I went home wondering what there was in γάνος which could not be expressed by 'sheen'. I looked it up and found '*Brightness, sheen, gladness, joy, pride*'.

We were soon acquainted, for we were in the same situation; each was in the position of having no more than a year in which to read the English School, for had we taken two we would have been overstanding for Honours. I had read the History School before, and he Honour Classical Mods and Greats. Apart from this similarity of situation, we shared the good fortune of having F. P. Wilson for our tutor in English literature, and all that year we lived at the rate of eight or ten working hours a day pressing forward under his unerring guidance, over the *terra incognita* (as it virtually was for us) of English poetry and prose. It was a continuous intoxication of discovery: to almost every week came its amazement. I remember particularly our excitement on first reading the poems of John Donne, who was just beginning, in those early years, to be known again after two centuries of contemptuous neglect. We were uninhibitedly happy in our work and felt supported by an endless energy.

There was no reason why we should not have been happy; we had both just emerged safely from a war which (we then believed) had ended war for ever. We had survived the trenches, the nightmare was over, we were at Oxford, we were in our early twenties. The old order seemed not only restored but renewed; life and art lay before us for exploration and the interchange of ideas, and we seemed to be experiencing what happened to Odin and his fellow-gods when they returned after their long twilight; finding their golden chessmen where they had left them in the grass, they sat down and went on with the game.

We saw clearly what lay before us, a life of reading and teaching, perhaps of writing—for, as we confessed to each other very soon, we both hoped to be poets, or at least writers. It was not until six or seven years later that Lewis said sadly to me, 'When I at last realized that I was not, after all, going to be a great man . . .' I think he meant 'a great poet'. In those early days however nothing seemed impossible as we fed our imaginations on all the best that had been written in our language; for it wonderfully illuminated, for both of us, the other subjects we had been studying up till then. In my case, all the history I had so painfully and uncomprehendingly imbibed for three years and more in the History School became suddenly intelligible to me in terms of its poetry. I had, for instance, taken the reign of Richard II as my special subject; but none of my history tutors had thought of suggesting anything so obvious as that I should read some Chaucer or Langland. I presume they took it for granted that I knew them already; so they were never mentioned, and I, in my ignorance, was virtually unaware of them. But now, while all that the chronicles and other sources had told me of the reign of Richard was still fresh in my head, the poetry of *The Canterbury Tales* and *Piers Plowman* suddenly added a new dimension to history for me: and these poems, of course, were no less vivified in their turn by what I knew of the fourteenth century. In the case of Lewis, he was finding all that he knew of Greek and

Latin poetry reflected in his English studies, and he was learning to illuminate the latter by the former with sudden comparisons and contrasts that sparkled and exploded in his conversation. I do not say these were anything new to the world, but they were new to *us* and gave excitement to our meetings: for we used to foregather in our rooms or go off for country walks together in endless but excited talk about what we had been reading the week before—for Wilson kept us pretty well in step with each other—and what we thought about it. So we would stride over Hinksey and Cumnor—we walked almost as fast as we talked—disputing and quoting, as we looked for the dark dingles and the tree-topped hills of Matthew Arnold. This kind of walk must be among the commonest, perhaps among the best, of undergraduate experiences. Lewis, with the gusto of a Chesterton or a Belloc, would suddenly roar out a passage of poetry that he had newly discovered and memorized, particularly if it were in Old English, a language novel and enchanting to us both for its heroic attitudes and crashing rhythms; it was he who first made me feel the force of poetry in the speech of Byrhtnoth, at the end of *The Battle of Maldon*, that begins

> Hige sceal þe heardra, heorte þe cenre,
> mod sceal þe mare, þe ure maegen lytlað . . .

as his big voice boomed it out with all the pleasure of tasting a noble wine. And then he was off on a comparison with some passage (not known to me) in the *Iliad*, using the two poems to epitomize their two civilizations with a grand sweep of generalization, that was later to be so distinctive a character of his critical work.

His tastes were essentially for what had magnitude and a suggestion of myth: the heroic and the romantic never failed to excite his imagination and although, at that time, he was something of a professed atheist, the mythically supernatural things in ancient epic and saga always attracted him. Here again his feeling for the Classics fed his romanticism and the gods were realities for him in the imaginative world, though he rejected God in his philosophical and practical worlds, at that time. This rejection in no way that I could sense diminished his delight in *Paradise Lost*; we had, of course, thunderous disagreements and agreements, and none more thunderous or agreeing than over *Samson Agonistes*, which neither of us had read before and which we reached, both together, in the same week; we found we had chosen the same passages as our favourites, and for the same reasons—the epic scale of their emotions and their overmastering rhythmical patterns; the two I remember him particularly to have quoted were:

> While their hearts were jocund and sublime,
> Drunk with idolatry, drunk with wine
> And fat regorged of bulls and goats . . . (*etc*)

and

> O dark, dark, dark, amid the blaze of noon,
> Irrecoverably dark, total eclipse
> Without all hope of day!

Yet when I tried to share with him my discovery of Restoration comedy he would have none of it. I pleaded for Congreve, asserting that there was a place for the Mirabellian worldling, the gentleman of wit, who might seem an apostate from romance, but who had a secret vision of love, however elaborately disavowed; there was a place for poise, for reserve, for a polished contempt: God would think twice before damning a man of that quality. But Lewis only had to think once, and in later years, when he had come round to Christianity, he had even less use or liking for Congreve and Co, as I remember. In a letter, once, he drew me a picture, or allegorical diagram, imitated from the well-known frontispiece of Hobbes's *Leviathan*, which showed a Leviathan of human values. In the head there stood a figure labelled SAINT. In the heart, a figure labelled HERO. Twittering round the huge figure there was an insect-like object dressed as a man of fashion of the seventeenth century and labelled GENTLEMAN; from its mouth their issued a balloon in which was written in tiny letters: '*and where do I come in?*'. Mirabel, he went on to say, was no part of the Everlasting Gospel, a phrase of Blake's that he had his own meaning for. Perhaps the hunger for magnitude that made him admire *Gilgamesh* and the *Edda*, and made Spenser and Milton his favourites, disabled him from an appreciation, which I could not deny, for a world of elegant cuckoldry and cynic wit, so seemingly heartless, a trifler's scum of humanity that sought to be taken for its cream. I found it very enjoyable, but I do not remember ever to have heard Lewis quote Congreve, though he relaxed enough to enjoy Dryden's rapier-bludgeon at work on Shadwell.

He tended to avoid the theatre, as a result, I suppose, of some North of Ireland Protestant scunner against it. I do not believe I ever saw him at a University production, nor did I ever invite him to one, even of my own, for fear of obliging him to sacrifice disinclination to politeness. Yet upon one occasion he went to see a professional company perform *The Winter's Tale* and he came away overwhelmed by the experience. What he had thought a relatively dull, improbable, and unattractive play had been revealed to him by the theatre as a high romance, with a stern but admirable moral core given to it by the character of Paulina, and a myth-like renovation at the end, when the statue of Hermione melts back into life. He often expressed his amazement to me, after that, at the power of theatre to transfigure a play, and inject it with significances he could never have imagined without it: yet for all that, he did not change custom or become a theatregoer, and this, I think, was a part of the price he had to pay for a habit of Protestantism.

This was a rooted thing in him and gave colour even to his

atheism: it was a part of his formidableness; but he was first formidable in appearance, rather as Dr Johnson (to judge by Sir Joshua Reynolds) was formidable. There were many echoes of Johnson in Lewis. Both were formidable in their learning and in the range of their conversation, both had the same delight in argument, and in spite of their regard for truth, would argue for victory. Lewis had Johnson's handiness with the butt end of a pistol if an argument misfired. Like Johnson, he was a largish, unathletic-looking man, heavy but not tall, with a roundish, florid face that perspired easily and showed networks of tiny blood-vessels on close inspection; he had a dark flop of hair and rather heavily pouched eyes; these eyes gave life to the face, they were large and brown and unusually expressive. The main effects were of a mild, plain powerfulness, and over all there was a sense of simple masculinity, of a virility absorbed into intellectual life. He differed in his youth from most others of his age by seeming to have no sexual problems or preoccupations, or need to talk about them if he had them: and it was with surprise that I read of the 'brown girls' in his first prose work, *The Pilgrim's Regress*, whom the Pilgrim used to find lying beside him in the forest and which lured him on into thinking they could console him for, and even be more desirable than, the celestial city he was seeking.

His first 'brown girl' came in a different guise—not as a substitute for a heavenly reality, but as the climax and reward after an act of rebellion against authority, the history of which is given in his first, long poem, *Dymer*, which he showed me during the early days of our acquaintance, towards 1924. He had told me that he had been visited many years before by a dream or myth that had remained completely mysterious to him, and yet compelling. It held his imagination though he could not explain its significance. He had made a poem of it, he said. I asked him to let me see it, and presently it arrived, a thickish folder of typewritten cantos in rhyme-royal. It was the first time that I had been entrusted with an original work of such weight and I read it with all the excitement natural in one who is first privileged to see new work by a new poet.

The essence of the myth of *Dymer* is given in Lewis's own words in the introduction to the edition of 1950. He says it is 'the story of a man who, on some mysterious bride, begets a monster: which monster, as soon as it has killed its father, becomes a god'. The mysterious bride (though never described in the poem) is surely the first of the 'brown girls' that seem to console but make difficult the path of the poet. It is an up-rush of seemingly innocent sexuality that leads him to the for-fended place and to an ecstasy never, in the poem, recovered; for the mysterious bride vanishes as inexplicably as she has come, and instead, something ancient, female, and monstrous appears that bars Dymer's way, when he seeks her. Lewis tells us that we are at liberty to allegorize or psychoanalyse his story as we please. As far as he was concerned, at least in those early days, it had a felt significance which he could not under-stand or explain. I do not feel able to accept his invitation to allegorize or psychoanalyse it, but I confess to a feeling of significance in it which I cannot explain either.

Lewis tells us that he is aware of influences from Euripides, Milton, Morris, and the early Yeats that were potent among those that went to its creation. For myself, I cannot catch many of these echoes, but hear, strongly enough, the voice of Masefield, as I read the poem. It is a long romantic story, told like Mase-field's *Dauber*, in rhyme-royal, and it uses a like language which combines occasional racinesses of colloquial idiom with what may be called the Pre-Raphaelite idiom in its second or third generation, and a strong injection of Pre-Raphaelite stained glass imagery. None of this, perhaps, will please today, but in those early 'twenties, before the victories of the New Sensi-bility had become certain, Masefieldian romance and narrative manner were still appreciated, though the half-lyrical, half-elegiac and very fragmentary contemplations that compose *The Waste Land* had already appeared, and were establishing a very different kind of English out of the norms of intellectual conversation, and from imagery taken, not from Malory or Victorian romance, but from the decline of the West, the march of materialism and the unconscious.

Dymer has a toe-hold in Wardour Street and once this is perceived no merit it may have is likely wholly to save it: yet it is a good story well told, and supported by the sense of there being a powerful mind behind it, flashing out occasionally with an original expression, such as 'a thought that is still waiting to be thought', or in a well-sustained passage of natural description, in a vein that harks back to the countryside tradition of poetry and to the sentiment of nature, rather than to the vein of the poetry of conurbation that began with *The Love Song of J. Alfred Prufrock*. Faint echoes of Edward Thomas or Masefield, for instance, seem to make overtones to this stanza from *Dymer*:

> The same night swelled the mushroom in earth's lap
> And silvered the wet fields: it drew the bud
> From hiding and led on the rhythmic sap
> And sent the young wolves thirsting after blood,
> And, wheeling the big seas, made ebb and flood
> Along the shores of earth: and held these two
> In dead sleep till the time of morning dew.

Like Johnson, Lewis was more impressive in his conversation than in his poetry, and more impressive in his prose—particularly in his learned prose—than in his conversation. There is a magistral quality in the English of his finest work, to be seen in his volume on the sixteenth century in *The Oxford History of English Literature*—or in *The Allegory of Love* or in *Preface to Paradise Lost*. The marks of this style are weight and clarity of argument, sudden turns of generalization and genial paradox, the telling short sentence to sum a complex paragraph, and unexpected touches of personal approach to the reader, whom he always assumes to be as logical, as learned, as romantic, and as open to conviction as himself. Not that in fact he was easily open to conviction; perhaps 'open to argument' would be a truer description.

Underneath all, I sense in his style an indefeasible core of Protestant certainties, the certainties of a simple, unchanging, entrenched ethic that knows how to distinguish, unarguably, between Right and Wrong, Natural and Unnatural, High and Low, Black and White, with a committed force, an ethic on which his ramified and seemingly conciliatory structures of argument are invisibly based; but the strength that they derive from this hard core deprived him of certain kinds of sympathy and perception. He had little sympathy, as I have said, for Mirabel, and little for what I have called the New Sensibility of the early 'twenties, for its flat bleakness, its lawless versification, its unheroic tone, its unintelligible images, its 'modernity' in short. It delighted him that he could find no use of the word *modern* in Shakespeare that did not carry its load of contempt. The new psychology was another of the advances of 'modernity' that he regarded with suspicion. None of these things were a part of the everlasting gospel; they were the quirks of fretful foreigners to good sense, sound poetry, and the known stuff of the soul. He did not feel at home in the poetry of Mr Eliot or in that of the Sitwells; I do not remember ever to have heard him speak of the poetry of D. H. Lawrence or Ezra Pound. But of all older poets he spoke gladly, learnedly, and often paradoxically, throwing out powerful assertions that challenged discussion. I remember, on one occasion, as I went round Addison's Walk, I saw him coming slowly towards me, his round, rubicund face beaming with pleasure to itself. When we came within speaking distance, I said 'Hullo, Jack! You look very pleased with yourself; what is it?'

'I believe,' he answered, with a modest smile of triumph,

'I *believe* I have proved that the Renaissance never happened in England. *Alternatively*'—he held up his hand to prevent my astonished exclamation—'that if it did, *it had no importance!*'

He had the gift of a pungent simplicity in conversation, and this ability to make sudden, provocative generalizations. This simplicity and provocation will also be found in all his polemical prose and they seem to derive from the elements I have tried to describe in him. On one occasion he was dining with me in Exeter College, placed on the right of the Rector. Rector Marett was a man of abundant geniality and intelligence, always ready with friendly freshets of conversation and new gambits of gossip to entertain a guest. Presently he turned to Lewis and said:

'I saw in the papers this morning that there is some scientist-fellah in Vienna, called Voronoff—some name like that—who has invented a way of splicing the glands of young apes onto old gentlemen, thereby renewing their generative powers! Remarkable, isn't it?'

Lewis thought.

'I would say "unnatural".'

'Come, come! "Unnatural"! What do you mean, *"unnatural"*? Voronoff is a part of Nature isn't he? What happens in Nature must surely be natural? Speaking as a philosopher, don't you know'—(Marett taught Philosophy)—'I can attach no meaning to your objection; I don't understand you!'

'I am sorry, Rector; but I think any philosopher from Aristotle to—say—Jeremy Bentham, would have understood me.'

'Oh, well, we've got beyond Bentham by now, I hope. If Aristotle or he had known about Voronoff, they might have changed their ideas. Think of the possibilities he opens up! You'll be an old man yourself, one day.'

'*I would rather be an old man than a young monkey.*'

We all laughed at this pay-off line, but behind the wit and

the thinking-power lay the puritan strength; because he could also laugh, it seemed warm and humane; but it was unbending. He never gave quarter in debate and never lost his temper; he always argued with seriousness and drew on his learning—at times on very recondite learning—for argument, and on his ready imagination for analogies.

His conversion to Christianity seems to have come about largely by thinking, if we may believe his own account of it, given in *Surprised by Joy*. It did not come by sudden intuition, or overwhelming vision, or even by the more usual path of conviction of sin calling for repentance and atonement. It came by taking thought and it added many cubits to his stature. It opened to him an understanding (for instance) of forgiveness, a concept to which he had once told me (in his atheist days) he could attach no meaning—'unless it means that I am to pretend that something wicked you have done has never happened'. His Christianity, so important to him personally, was also important professionally, for it enabled him to enter into fuller imaginative sympathy with the Middle Ages and Renaissance (whether it existed or not) and give spiritual substance to his life's work in those fields, so penetrated by Christian thought. No one knew better than he how an understanding of poetry depends on an understanding of the poet's universe.

I think his Christianity gave ease to his camaraderie with some of his friends, who for the most part were Christians. Above all it made possible one of his most intimate friendships, which was with Charles Williams. It was my happiness to have introduced Lewis to Williams's work, of which he happened not to have heard, by lending him a copy of his extraordinary novel, *The Place of a Lion*. Lewis read it, was captivated by the strange blend of Plato and Genesis, wrote to Williams, met him, and introduced him to the Inklings (a group of us described in *Surprised by Joy*) to our great delight.

It was a group that met in each others' rooms from time to

time, and whenever any of us had written anything which he felt ready to read out to the others, he did so. So it came about that we were able to listen amazed to Williams's endearing cockney, as he stormed his way through *Taliessin through Logres*, and, when he had reached a conclusion, hear him say 'Well, I don't know if that is *pow*-etry, but that's how it comes to *me*!' (a roar of his laughter) 'Does it sound like pow-etry to *you*?' He and Lewis quickly became fast friends: they seemed to live in the same spiritual world. I believe Williams was the only one of us, except perhaps Ronald Tolkien, from whom Lewis learnt any of his thinking. It was Charles Williams who expounded to him the doctrine of co-inherence and the idea that one had power to accept into one's own body the pain of someone else, through Christian love. This was a power which Lewis found himself later to possess, and which, he told me, he had been allowed to use to ease the suffering of his wife, a cancer victim, of whom the doctors had despaired. This kind of life-giving generosity was another depth in Lewis's nature that was a part of his greatness, but I did not discover it for some years; for though his benefactions were immense, they were secret and I only heard of a few of them and by accident. They were all private and personal, so far as I know. He would certainly not wish them to be recorded or discussed. Much of Lewis's life was hidden from me; he almost never spoke about himself, in my hearing at least: though once, shortly after his marriage, when he brought his wife to lunch with me, he said to me, looking at her across the grassy quadrangle, 'I never expected to have, in my sixties, the happiness that passed me by in my twenties.' It was then that he told me of having been allowed to accept her pain.

'You mean' (I said) 'that her pain left her, and that you felt it for her in your body?'

'Yes,' he said, 'in my legs. It was crippling. But it relieved hers.'

In his last years, when he had gone to Cambridge, which he came to love so much as to prefer it to Oxford, he still kept his house on Headington Hill, by the old kilns and the little lakes where Shelley is said to have sailed paper boats. I used to visit him there from time to time. On one of the last occasions I found him writing an article for a popular American weekly. It is always interesting to know how a writer writes, and I asked him whether he had to make ten or twenty drafts (as I have to) of anything he wished to print. No, he said, he just made a rough copy, then corrected it and made a fair copy: and that was it. The gift of phrase was instantaneous in him, and that must partly account for his huge output; but there was a plentitude of mind as well as a swiftness of phrase to help him; he never put a nib wrong. I asked him how he came to be writing for the popular American weekly. How did he know what to write about or what to say? 'Oh,' he said, 'they have somehow got the idea that I am an unaccountably paradoxical dog, and they name the subject on which they want me to write; and they pay generously.' 'And so you set to work and invent a few paradoxes?' 'Not a bit of it. What I do is to recall, as well as I can, what my mother used to say on the subject, eke it out with a few similar thoughts of my own, and so produce what would have been strict orthodoxy in about 1900. And this seems to them outrageously paradoxical, *avant garde* stuff.' I then recalled having read a copy of *Time Magazine* in which some naïve reviewer had been taken aback when Lewis, asked if the quiet routine of his life was not somewhat monotonous, had replied, '*I like monotony.*' This truism was a kind of paradox unthinkable to *Time Magazine*. On another occasion he was asked what he thought of the Hydrogen Bomb. He said he could not see that it made any difference; the world had been expecting to come suddenly and painfully to an immediate end since at least the eleventh century, as anyone who had read Wulfstan would realize; 'and anyhow, when the bomb falls there will always be just that split second in which one can say "Pooh! you're only a bomb. I'm an immortal soul"'. Ulster, Greece, Rome, Oxford, and Cambridge were in that joke.

Though I miss him much as a man, I miss him most because of the loss of his living force in the kind of study in which we were both engaged, the study of English, of which he was easily the greatest teacher of our time in his chosen fields; but thousands will remember him with delight for his other kinds of writing, his space-travel, his theology, his books for children. It may be that the *Chronicles of Narnia* may outlive *The Allegory of Love*, and *Perelandra* outlive them both. Few works of learning and criticism survive a hundred years; what it was learned to know in 1950 will be expected of scholarship-candidates in 2000; new things will be discovered, old notions disproved, other critical values asserted: but a piece of genuine imagination in fiction may have a long life.

Nevertheless his critical work has the unusual qualities of his mind at large, of which I think the chief to be his power to read and enjoy fluently in five or six languages: the power to think; the power to make judgments and generalizations that lead the reader into new territory: the power to write quickly, clearly, and with colour and force. His sentences are in homely English, and yet there is something Roman in the easy handling of clauses, and something Greek in their ascent from analogy to idea. The subjects he has chosen to write on have generally been of intrinsic greatness and difficulty; in the field of literature he has illuminated a whole way of sexual feeling in *The Allegory of Love*, a whole age of poetry and prose in *The Sixteenth Century*, a major poet in *Preface to Paradise Lost* and a forgotten universe in *The Discarded Image*: these are magistral books and I do not know of any critic of our times who can equal this achievement. Almost any page of almost any of them will yield sentences that a critical writer may envy, and I take a specimen from his last book to show this mastery:

E

Whatever else a modern feels when he looks at the night sky, he certainly feels that he is looking *out*—like one looking out from the saloon entrance on to the dark Atlantic or from the lighted porch upon dark and lonely moors. But if you accepted the Mediaeval Model you would feel like one looking *in*. The Earth is 'outside the city wall'. When the sun is up he dazzles us and we cannot see inside. Darkness, our own darkness, draws the veil and we catch a glimpse of the high pomps within; the vast, lighted concavity filled with music and life. And, looking in, we do not see, like Meredith's Lucifer, 'the army of unalterable law', but rather the revelry of insatiable love. We are watching the activity of creatures whose experience we can only lamely compare to that of one in the act of drinking, his thirst delighted yet not quenched. For in them the highest of faculties is always exercised without impediment on the noblest object; without satiety, since they can never completely make His perfection their own, yet never frustrated, since at every moment they approximate to Him in the fullest measure of which their nature is capable. . . .

This has weight of vision and definition of style. Whoever thinks justly of him will find him impressive, and he was always impressive to meet; I prefer my first word, 'formidable'. But this was softened by joviality in youth and kindliness in maturity. Genius is formidable and so is goodness; he had both. It is useful in a picture sometimes to introduce a balancing figure to give scale, and I would choose the figure of W. H. Auden as one of comparable impressiveness and goodness, felt as formidable and friendly. Learning, of course, can never weigh equally with poetry, and so Lewis at once tips the beam; but Lewis has much poetry, and Auden has much learning; both have greatness. I believe that when they met, they liked each other. I wish I had been there.

4

The Tutor and the Scholar

BY

JOHN LAWLOR

'Wʜᴀᴛ ᴍᴏsᴛ eludes description is not the excellence of his gifts but the singularity of his essential being.' So Housman wrote of his colleague Arthur Platt; and the words are wholly applicable to Lewis. There was, to begin with, the discrepancy between what one expected of the accomplished medieval scholar (and, later, the penetrating exponent of theological and spiritual matters) and the robust, no-nonsense, unmistakably strident man, clumsy in movement and in dress, apparently little sensitive to the feelings of others, determined to cut his way to the heart of any matter with shouts of *distinguo!* before re-shaping it entirely. One quickly felt that for him dialectic supplied the place of conversation. Any general remarks were of an obvious and even platitudinous kind; talk was dead timber until the spark of argument flashed. Then in a trice you were whisked from the particular to fundamental principles; thence (if you wanted) to eternal verities; and Lewis was alert for any riposte you could muster. It was comic as well as breathtaking; and Lewis would see the comedy as readily as the next man. He was, of course, only passing on what he had learned from 'the Great Knock'. As we may learn from *Surprised by Joy*, the young Lewis was at first as dismayed as any of his own pupils at a conversational technique indistinguishable from *viva voce* examination. But he learned quickly; and before long the instructor was commending the pupil. In this regard, Lewis never looked back. He was the dialectician all his life; and one must only add that he was superb. Lewis on form (and I do not remember him ever being much below form) was a Black Belt among novices. There was a memorable occasion when in the Hall at Magdalen Dr Tillyard met him to round off in debate the controversy begun with the publication of Lewis's indictment of 'the Personal Heresy'. I am afraid there was no debate. Lewis made rings round Tillyard; in, out, up, down, around, back again—like some piratical Plymouth bark against a high-built galleon of Spain. Never was there a more skilful demonstration of 'the Great Knock's' skills. As to the issues of the debate, that, perhaps, is another story. There is no doubt that immense dialectical skill can batter an opponent into silence. But, as Adam Fox once reminded us, in the words of Daniel Waterland, 'It is one thing to understand the doctrine, and quite another to be masters of the controversy.' Lewis's ambition was of course to know the doctrine and to be master of the controversy.

I first met Lewis in October 1936. My notion of Oxford, and Oxford dons, was firmly preconceived: for three years I was to pursue truth in a setting of architectural and spiritual refinement. Dons to me were sports-jacketed figures with pastel ties, reclining under the great chestnut-tree at Balliol in apparent indolence, but all the while razor-keen to detect inconsistencies in attitude or standpoint. I say 'attitude or standpoint' since formal argument held little appeal. I agreed, of course, that some of the inconsistencies we were after could be approached ratiocinatively, and examined for logical contradiction; but the deeper kinds of awareness were to be reached intuitively rather than through rationalizations. This in fact constituted my justification for studying imaginative literature at all, rather than history or philosophy or psychology. I held that when one sensed (rather than 'detected') a defect of style, a false emphasis of rhythm, or an inadequate characterization, one was at that point gaining insight into the real subject of enquiry, through the gap between the thing made and its potentiality; and from that point one must go forward and into the work, not outward into analogy and speculation, however brilliant. What I was looking for was not a methodology but a way of life, one which would encourage and sustain a maximum receptivity to works of art. I knew (or thought I knew) enough about 'reality' in the sense of quotidian experience—though there, too, I wanted heightened awareness, not escape into fantasy or moralized judgment.

Lewis lived in as good a setting as any man for the life of vigilant aestheticism I had pictured for myself. His rooms were on the first floor of New Buildings 3, and ran the width of the building, so that the sitting-room looked out on Magdalen Grove, the other half of the suite commanding the Cloister, and, in the background, the incomparable Tower. My first tap on the door drew a bellowed 'Come in!', and there was my mentor for the next three years—red-faced, bald (the dark flop Coghill speaks of had gone), dressed in baggy jacket and trousers (alas! no pastel tie), and obviously in no mood to waste time—a permanent characteristic, I found. For my first Term I read Pass Moderations—bits of Constitutional Law and History, Pliny's *Letters*, some English literature (Dryden's *Essay of Dramatic Poesy* came in, I remember), and, as a preparation for an English School solidly ranged on principles Lewis staunchly upheld, some elementary Anglo-Saxon. The tuition for all except the Anglo-Saxon would come from others: with Lewis one did the grammar from Sweet's *Primer* and worked up from the early sentences to the piece on King Edmund. I remember only two things about the Anglo-Saxon sessions. One was the suggested translation of *Eala þu biscop* as

'Tut! tut! Your Grace'; the other was my first experience of Lewis's determined impersonality towards all except his very closest friends. I had clean forgotten to come to an extra class which Lewis had generously offered; and I afterwards went to see him with real regret at having been so stupid. He cut short my apologies: 'I'm not your schoolmaster, you know.' It was coldly said, and coldly meant. If I couldn't keep to the appointed duties of an undergraduate (they were few enough, heaven knows) then doubtless I would sooner or later have to go. But I mustn't think of our relationship as a *personal* one.

With the Hilary Term we started on the English School proper, and here Lewis was in his element—the more so as, of the choices offered, I had decided to begin with Spenser. The tutorial ritual was always the same. The pupil, gowned and clutching his essay (an affair of some 3,000 words or more) sat on the comfortable but shapeless settee. Lewis, smoking vigorously (I never saw him without pipe or cigarettes except when eating or out on a walk) sat in the armchair, pencil in hand; and there he doodled, caricatured, and made an occasional note, while the pupil read aloud (twenty minutes might be an average time). Then Lewis would proceed to an examination of what was said; and often, what was not said. I once reminded him of Ronald Knox's remark: 'The prevailing attitude . . . was one of heavy disagreement with a number of things which the reader had not said.' The point was taken; the more the pupil showed a capacity for self-defence the better Lewis was pleased. I like to think that he enjoyed some of our tutorials; for the plain fact is that he hated teaching. The reasons for this are not far to seek. In the first place, as a young don (and on into early middle age), Lewis got relatively few pupils in English, and those were of varying quality. In these days of rapid expansion, with English often leading all others in undergraduate numbers, it requires an effort of imagination to realize how few read the Oxford English School in the between wars years; and, frankly, before the days of 'practical criticism' in the schools, how dreadfully amateurish we could be. At Magdalen, one of the larger Oxford Colleges, and one of the few to have a Tutorial Fellow in English, the number of freshmen in 1936 proposing to read English was precisely two: and this is not untypical of the period. In consequence, part of Lewis's tutorial duties was to teach Political Science to Magdalen undergraduates reading History and Modern Greats; and in addition he had a lectureship at Univ., his old College, which he held until Dyson took it over in, I think, 1946. Secondly, Lewis's own temperament and interests led him very far from any conviction that the study of imaginative literature, even when undertaken by first-rate intelligences, could justify some of the exalted claims made for it. He was correspondingly ready to open the range of the pupil's mind, given fair opportunity. Where he could not strike fire, he tended to accept with ironic resignation; but it did not endear teaching to him. Thirdly—and I have, I believe, kept the true order of importance—Lewis valued time as few men I have met, before or since, have done. After an early breakfast and a walk, nine o'clock in Term time would see him seated at his writing-table, wooden penholder and steel nib moving steadily over the page until the ten o'clock pupil knocked on his door. 'The hungry generations tread thee down' was a witticism he ruefully acknowledged. No man was better equipped for silent industry, hour upon hour; and, after the war especially, when undergraduates of all ages flocked into the university, few men had more calls upon their time, not only for tutorial duties but to address the clubs and societies which sprang up on every hand. To Lewis, tutorial work was a school of patience; and if one was ever disappointed that one's best things had gone unregarded, one was also conscious that one's best wasn't good enough to feed and sustain his most remarkable mind.

The effect of this was that a good many of Lewis's pupils,

including the very best of them, were reduced to silence or, worse, incoherence when dealing with him. It is one thing to 'admit captivity by a higher and nobler mind'; another to find something to say to pass the rest of the hour. Lewis's gifts, then, as a tutor, strike me as representative of both the virtues and the defects of the Oxford tutorial system as it was practised in my time. For some it would prove an unmatched experience in intellectual exhilaration—a sight of wide horizons and a growing sense of 'The achieve of, the mastery of the thing'. For others, unhappy silence on the part of the pupil, while Lewis would boom away in unavailing efforts to draw a response, or eventually fall silent in turn. Neither category of pupil corresponds neatly with the able and the mediocre-to-weak. Men of high ability would find nothing to say: and men of less ability might cheerfully forge ahead, to make a series of passes which the veteran could joyously beat down, while crying his approval. One thing Lewis never did, in all my recollection of him. He never imposed his Christianity on the argument. If it was there already (and the great majority of writers we were dealing with were Christian in their cast of mind if not always in any direct allegiance) he would take up the point and develop it. But never would he obtrude his beliefs. Here, as in all other aspects of his life, he was reserved to an almost fantastic degree. The determined and even aggressive joviality was all on the surface: within was a settled contentment, guarded by a schoolboy's contempt for 'pi-jaw'.

As for me, I passed from dislike and hostility to stubborn affection, and then to gratitude for the weekly bout in which no quarter was asked or given. Lewis's own account, in the preface to *Essays presented to Charles Williams*, of 'the cut and parry of prolonged, fierce, masculine argument' perfectly characterizes his notion of a good tutorial. It happened that I had ready-made what Lewis as a young don had found necessary to adopt, a position to argue from. His, as he describes it in *Surprised by*

Joy was 'watered Hegelianism'; mine, hastily acquired in the sixth form and maintained but not adequately scrutinized until the end of my second year at Oxford, was dialectical materialism—'Hegel the right way up.' (It showed, by the way, the degree of open-mindedness he practised that he chose me for a Magdalen award, with my clamantly socialist papers before him, when I had thought of myself as God's gift to Lindsay's Balliol, with which Magdalen was teamed for scholarship purposes.) In my first Term I met a kindred spirit in Robert Conquest and together we founded the Ralph Fox group —Magdalen's first left-wing socialist society. It was the time of the Spanish Civil War, and we were busy in organizing lunches for refugee funds, collecting money by point-blank asking, and getting up meetings and demonstrations in support of the Spanish Government. I must have been the last man Lewis wanted to see. He valued above all else his privacy, and here was I invading it with requests to give money or to join in meetings of the liberally-minded. It must have hurt him very much to refuse money. The scale of his benefactions will perhaps never be known; but he was surely one of the most cheerful givers, according to his means, who ever lived. He could not contribute to anything that had a directly political implication; but I did get a paper out of him when he inaugurated the English Society (a venture which came from my and others' dissatisfaction with an English Club that perpetually devoted itself to such notable English writers as Blok, George, Rilke, *et al.*).

The paper ('Our English Syllabus') expresses perfectly the spirit of Lewis's tutoring: 'The student is, or ought to be, a young man who is already beginning to follow learning for its own sake, and who attaches himself to an older student, not precisely to be taught, but to pick up what he can.' ('I'm not your schoolmaster, you know.') There were, however, certain things that weren't to be picked up, notably modern literature.

Anyone, Lewis declared contemptuously in the same paper, 'who wants a tutor's assistance in reading the works of his own contemporaries might as well ask for a nurse's assistance in blowing his own nose'. These were, I may add, the days (not so long distant, at that) when the farthest reach into modernity dared by the Oxford syllabus was 1830. Lewis had not the least conception of Eliot's view that we need the past in order to understand the present—much less its corollary, that the present, fairly confronted, will enable us to understand the past. He was fond of maintaining that the present was itself 'only a period' (a bad one, in his view); but he was not prepared to see the past as only a period. The paper on the English syllabus should be read along with its companion-piece (both are printed in *Rehabilitations*), 'The Idea of an "English School"'. There, with characteristic humour, Lewis indicates his own conservative position under the appropriate image of trench warfare. 'I do not know,' he says, 'where the last ditch in our educational war may be at the moment; but point it out to me on the trench-map and I will go to it.'

Against this redoubtable conservatism I pitted myself in the weekly tutorial. The disparity between our armament could hardly be greater—his howitzer opposed to my pea-shooter. But to it we went—with increasing goodwill on his side and growing respect on mine. How could a materialist like me have anything on which to base the notion of value? What was the final stage of the supposedly continuous dialectic of history? Could there be an ultimate 'synthesis'? Why, if it was inevitable, should we contend for it, much less approve it? The reader may think these were poor English tutorials, perhaps deserving Lewis's own strictures, in *The Abolition of Man*, on 'the work of amateur philosophers', when it is substituted for that of 'professional grammarians'. The reader would be wrong. It was all in the course of business. Week by week I read my essays on Milton or Dryden or Johnson, and week by week we joined battle—sometimes an indolent grenade or two, some times all-out offensive. I was allowed the initiative on every occasion; Lewis gave me the choice of ground and of weapons —and of course beat me every time. But towards the end of the second year, when we had moved into later medieval literature, I found him prepared to accept more of my literary contentions than he had done before. On my side, philoso-phically, I was moving towards a kind of socialism which could be described as enlightened self-interest with a strong bias towards left-of-centre political action. *Language, Truth, and Logic* had appeared, and it left no room for either his ideal-ism or my own thorough-going materialism. By the middle of my third year I was actually interesting him. I remember, in particular, his approval of my maintaining the non-realistic nature of a large part of Shakespearian characterization. Like any good tutor he showed me how the case I had sketched could be made stronger, introducing me to an area of criticism, which, while it gave comforting support to my argument, seemed to him largely misconceived. By the end of my time as his pupil, I won't say that the cycle of Old Knock and young Lewis had wholly repeated itself. There was still far too much in my position that he thought mistaken, and I had made too little advance in dialectics. But the day did come, many years later, when Lewis cried halt. 'You're too quick for me,' he said, one golden morning in a Headington pub garden. One more instance of his generosity.

Those who did not know Lewis as a tutor may catch a glimpse in his own Dr Dimble (*That Hideous Strength*), inter-rupted in a matter of real importance by 'my dullest pupil, just ringing the bell . . . I must go to the study and listen to an essay on Swift beginning "Swift was born". Must try to keep my mind on it, too, which won't be easy.' There is all of Lewis in that, not forgetting the willed attention to the mediocre performer. For anyone who thought, however hazily, that the study of English literature was to consist in conscientious excerpting from standard authors, while juggling accepted phrases of approbation, he was a shock and a tonic. Coghill's word 'formidable' is absolutely right. Yet he was not out to shock—least of all by denigrating his authors. It was for this reason, indeed, that he viewed supervision at Cambridge, in some of its most renowned practitioners, with considerable reserve. The Oxford tutor, I seem to remember him saying, on first encounter with his pupil, asks, 'What have you been reading?'; and he follows on from there, taking the book and showing its virtues as well as its limitations, to lead in openminded enquiry to those who have been called major writers. The virtues, be it noted: Lewis had no use for mere 'debunking', least of all when it started with an unargued superiority of 'modern' (in no strictly examined sense) against 'ancient' or (worse) 'medieval'. But the Cambridge supervisor, he said, was likely to receive the answer to the same first question ('What have you been reading?') with the menacing words, 'Oh, you've been reading *that*, have you . . .' and then proceed to the knife-work of murdering to dissect, in order to sweep the vile body aside to make room for the certified masterpieces. There was generosity in Lewis's protest: he saw no justification for vilifying the dead. When he characterized, in his *Experiment in Criticism*, the kind of critic for whom the great names of the past 'are as so many lamp-posts for a dog', he really did mean 'lamp-post', a light shining out over the dwelling places of civilized man.

I could as readily as anyone deplore the influence of 'the Great Knock': his meeting with Lewis was perhaps one of the least fortunate in intellectual history. The shy boy from Belfast, making his naïve comments on the Surrey countryside, became the one who had no small talk; who talked habitually, as Johnson did, for victory. But never was there a more magnanimous victor. At times he could give the impression of conceit ('I am as conceited as the next man,' he cheerfully wrote), or even arrogance. But he had few illusions about himself, and none about his standing. He wrote to me, not long after inaugurating the Medieval and Renaissance Professorship, 'my medieval mission at Cambridge is, so far, a *flop d'estime*'. Self-conscious, yes: but self-deluded, never. I count it the greatest good fortune to have sorted out my intellectual equipment, once a week in Term-time for three years, under his vigilant and genial eye.

As to his scholarship, while it is true, as some have said, that the veriest freshman of the future will take for granted what was striking innovation in its own day, there is yet a very small class of books for which a future can be predicted. They are those works which handle a large subject—large not in range, merely, but in significance to the human spirit—with a pioneer's skill, marking out new country and leaving an indelible impression for all subsequent settlement of the area. They can be wrongheaded in approach or mistaken in detail; but they must be not so much accounts of literature in the past as themselves instances of literature in being. When Anatole France spoke of literary criticism as recording the adventures of the soul among masterpieces he doubtless had something of the sort in mind. Alas! from the ordinary output of criticism we can only conclude that there are some very dull souls about. Yet there is a rare category of works of criticism that justifies the aphorism. One thinks of Bradley's *Shakespearian Tragedy*, Ker's *Epic and Romance*, John Livingston Lowes's *Road to Xanadu*, to name no others. Each is a book which not only shows great powers of penetration and organizing skill; each succeeds in communicating the activity of a mind of the highest quality entirely intent on the material before it, to which it is giving new and distinctive shape. Let us describe these books in one word: they are all in the highest degree readable. Lewis's *The Allegory of Love* surely belongs in any such classification. There is a luminous intelligence of the first order at work—an angel who writes as only Lewis could, humorously, graphically, and with an exalted seriousness. To be sure, there are things to be disputed, in Lewis's book as in all the others of its distinguished class. Lewis was the first to point them out. On a Collection paper in which I had adopted, too uncritically for him, his view of the medieval antithesis between love and marriage, he himself wrote in parody of me, 'Mr Lewis seems to forget that Palamon and Arcite both wanted to *marry* Emelye.' But, as with the other works I have listed, here is a *book*, obedient to the first rule of writing—that on every page it asks to be read. How many extended works of literary criticism are truly unputdownable? It is the severest test; and *The Allegory of Love* triumphantly survives it. Lewis's *Sixteenth Century* volume in the Oxford History has its share of the same qualities; one thinks particularly of the passages on Dunbar, on Sidney, and, of course, on Spenser. But the plan of the series forbids the sweep of the earlier work. Lewis is at his best in linking the beliefs and assumptions of widely separated periods—a quality once again apparent in *The Discarded Image*, where we have one of the very few books to give insight into the intellectual and spiritual framework of the past without degenerating into tedious résumé and the laborious multiplying of instances.

I am not so fond of his *Preface to Paradise Lost*, which I take to be a magistral example (none better in its sweep or cogency) of what, on Lewis's own showing, in *The Personal Heresy*, lies outside the scope of evaluative criticism—the presumed intentions and working purposes of an author. But that book contains what to me is the most remarkable single piece of criticism in Lewis's entire output—the brilliant account of Virgil as one who 'added a new dimension to poetry'. Who can forget the characterization of Aeneas as 'a ghost of Troy until he becomes the father of Rome', or the masterly treatment of Virgil's sense of vocation 'in the double character of a duty and a desire'? I mention the chapter, too, for the remarkable skill Lewis had as a translator, particularly from Latin. A hundred examples from all over his published works leap to mind. Among the high-spirited there is the translation of the *Concilium in Monte Romarici* into rhyming couplets:

> The reader of that gospel gay
> Was Sister Eva, who (they say)
> Understands the practick part
> Of the Amatory Art . . .

Or the translation and comment on Prudentius's

> Os quoque parce
> Erigit et comi moderatur gaudia vultu,

which becomes

> Uplifts her face
> With moderated cheer, and civil looks
> Tempering her joy.

('Nothing,' adds Lewis, 'could suggest more vividly the smirk of a persevering governess who has finally succeeded in getting a small boy into trouble with his father.') Among the *tours de force* must be placed the translation of two extended passages from Alanus de Insulis into sixteenth-century prose, and a 'Middle English' rendering from Chrétien's *Lancelot* (both in *The Allegory of Love*); or, even, the style of speech given Merlin in *That Hideous Strength*, to represent 'the Latin of a man to whom Apuleius and Martianus Capella were the primary classics and whose elegances resembled those of the *Hisperica Famina*'. The motive in all this was not idle virtuosity. When he came to write his volume in the *Oxford History of English Literature*, Lewis consistently turned his neo-Latin authors into sixteenth-century English—'not simply', as he said, 'for the fun of it,' but to guard the reader from a false impression he might otherwise receive. When passages from Calvin, Scaliger, or Erasmus in modern English jostle passages from vernacular writers with all the flavour of their period about them, it is fatally easy to get the feeling that the Latinists are somehow more enlightened, less remote, less limited by their age, than those who wrote English. It seemed worth some pains to try to remove so serious and so latent a misconception.

If few had been sensitive enough to perceive this defect, inherent in the historical study of literature, there were even less who had the wit and scholarship to remedy it. The mere snobbery of 'modernity' was a life-long concern with Lewis. What he said in the preface to *The Allegory of Love*, in dedicating the book to his friend Owen Barfield ('wisest and best' of his 'unofficial teachers') records a major debt. He had been taught 'not to patronize the past, and . . . to see the present as itself a "period"'. I have already suggested the limitation in this: for him all periods were equal, but some were more equal than others. Yet when he spoke out against the present it was against what he took to be not presuppositions but manifest errors. His constant state, as tutor and scholar, is best described in what he wrote of himself on receiving Tillyard's rejoinder to his original foray on 'the personal heresy'. He was a man 'hungry for rational opposition'. Provided you gave him that, you had his interest; then, I think invariably, his friendship; and with it his lasting affection and instant readiness to help in any way he could.

It is not for me to speak in detail of either his theological writings or his narrative fiction. All his work, though, is of one piece; and two of his narratives throw particular light on his interests in literary study. I have spoken rather slightingly of his *Preface to Paradise Lost* for what it has to say about Milton. But what it tells us of Lewis's own exalted imagination is finely complemented in *Perelandra*, where once again a Fall, it seems, is to be re-enacted; but this time there is a happy turn—a *eucatastrophe*, to use a word of Tolkien's which Lewis admired. It is good to know that we may some time hear an operatic version of this remarkable work. There is one other piece of narrative to be mentioned, and I would place it above all others. *Till We Have Faces* is truly a 'myth' in the sense which Lewis himself defined in his *Experiment in Criticism*—a story which 'depends hardly at all on such usual narrative attractions as suspense or surprise' and communicates the sense of that which is 'not only grave but awe-inspiring'. For once, Lewis attained something which he approved above all else and for which he revered *Comus*, a 'dearly bought singleness of quality—

> smooth and full as if one gush
> Of life had washed it'.

To say so much is of course very far from suggesting that the other writings are not worthy of close attention. I can claim to have read almost every word that Lewis published, and I find myself re-reading a good deal of the narrative fiction. Had anyone before C. P. Snow described a College meeting more vividly than Lewis in *That Hideous Strength*? How well one knows 'the Progressive Element', including its puppet-leader Curry, a sub-Warden 'so used to superintending the lives of his colleagues that it came naturally to him to superintend their deaths'. The children's books, again, show a power inherent in all the best of Lewis's critical writing—to communicate with complete simplicity a world of unspoilt nature. No argument here; only that 'quiet fullness of ordinary nature' which Lewis honoured in George Macdonald.

The phrase stands at the head of the final chapter of *The Allegory of Love*. In Lewis's own life a 'quiet fullness' meant that the transcendental was never at variance with the prosaic.

F

When 'Joy' came, while it 'made all my erotic and magical perversions of Joy look like sordid trumpery, it had no such disenchanting power over the bread upon the table or the coals in the grate'. There was no split in Lewis's personality, as some liked to imagine, between the strong sense of fact and the region of high imagination. I have written elsewhere[1] on the 'romantic theology' which Lewis shared with and in part learned from Charles Williams. The status it gives to heightened awareness of the external world is, I believe, a step forward in man's understanding of his complex nature. Certainly in Lewis himself the visionary and the moralist, commonly disjoined, are at one.

It is as certain as these things can be that we shall not see another like him—at least, in making the same intellectual voyage. The record he gave in *Pilgrim's Regress* was, as he later wryly admitted, based upon incomprehension of the modern mind. 'I committed the same sort of blunder as one who should narrate his travels through the Gobi Desert on the assumption that this route was as familiar to the British public as the line from Euston to Crewe.' But if his work in English studies is to be advanced, two starting-points offer themselves for re-investigation—medieval *fyne amour*, and rebellious romanticism. Each was in some measure an opponent of, and each became in some degree a successful usurper on, the fullness of religious experience. *Fyne amour* stands over against religion apprehended primarily as morality, emergent romanticism challenges religion as the revelation of final reality. I sometimes imagine a single book that would synthesize Lewis's life-work as an English scholar. It might begin with eighteenth century antiquarian interest in the middle ages, and by comparing the imagined or 'Gothick' past with the real Middle Ages it would recover some of the ground lost to abstraction and simplica-

[1] *Friendship's Garland: Essays presented to Mario Praz*, Edizioni di Storia e Letteratura, Rome 1966.

tion in that first scholarly debate. It would then survey poetical appropriation of this imagined past, from the high noon of Coleridge and Keats up to the death of romantic individualism in the middle and later nineteenth century, when the former rebels, Coleridge and Newman prominent among them, embrace a Christianity which finds little place for exalted awareness of the external world. The course of the argument, so far, would be to show, firstly, the identification of heightened experience with longing for a supposedly lost 'world of fine fabling', piquant and arresting because unalterably removed from actuality; secondly, this bitter-sweet experience of longing becoming at the hands of major poets the touchstone of all signficance, the evidence of 'Imagination, awful Power'. Now the setting and apparatus, all the legacy of 'the fairy way of writing', offers itself to the poet as the perfect medium for what is otherwise inexpressible—precisely because every tincture of belief in its objective existence has gone. 'A frightful fiend' can be the embodiment of nameless dread only when no fiend is to be met in reality. This part of the book would amply demonstrate Lewis's own recognition that the old gods had to die before 'they could wake again in the beauty of acknowledged myth'. The myth, in turn, flies at the touch of a colder religion. Did not Newman say that his soul was like glass in transmitting the warmth of faith to others, itself remaining cold? The third part of our investigation might point forward past this death to another re-awakening, this time in the present century, when T. S. Eliot, the former opponent of romanticism (and on that score one of Lewis's earlier targets) comes to celebrate a Christianity that ascends from penitential sadness to a final certainty, when reason and imagination are no longer at variance:

> And all shall be well and
> All manner of thing shall be well
> When the tongues of flame are in-folded

> Into the crowned knot of fire
> And the fire and the rose are one.

It is of course a book that would run counter to many established half-truths and as such have to contest every inch of the way. But then—to quote one of Lewis's supreme poets—it always was so:

> Sed revocare gradum superasque evadere ad auras,
> Hoc opus, hic labor est.

As to the man himself, Coghill suggests that a balancing figure may give scale. My comparison is with one who was no less remarkable for goodness, though temperamentally as different as could be. K. J. Spalding, of Brasenose, was the gentlest of men—utterly incapable of finding fault, generous in the highest degree, both in the range of his spirit and in openhanded benefaction, and altogether a stranger to that region of strong ratiocination and dogmatic assertion in which Lewis gloried. It was my happiness to bring them together at dinner. Lewis, I thought, put on one of his least tolerable performances; he was restless, assertive, and talking for effect. (There was, I now think, much on his mind at the time.) But Spalding saw immediately his goodness of heart, drew him amiably aside from his trumpeting certainties, and brought out of him, as the rest of us listened, the real warmth and vigour of a mind which I have not seen equalled.

Perhaps a harmless fantasy may finally be allowed. Lewis would have allowed it, anyway: 'laughing to teach the truth, what hinders?' After he had gone to Cambridge I used to entertain the conjecture that in a mishearing of names, those who sought spiritual certainties would be directed to Mr Leavis; and those who desired to know the unshakeable verities of literary study would find themselves confronted by Lewis. Who would in any way be the loser? In Mr Leavis enquirers would find intent self-appraisal: and in Lewis?—those robust certainties which must force the listener to look well to his own defences. What Barfield said in dedicating his *Poetic Diction* to 'Clive Hamilton' will serve as the experience of anyone who, refusing to be swept off his feet by Lewis, would stay to learn from him. 'Opposition' was, indeed, 'true friendship'.

5

Imaginative Writing

BY

STELLA GIBBONS

ENGLISH PEOPLE have always enjoyed stories about marvels. Perhaps we began to value cosiness early in our history, when firelight seemed brighter and warmer because of the dim weeping weather outside, and the wonder-full, awesome tale told round the hearth had the same effect.

The imaginative tale winds through the gay and bloody, red, white, and blue patterns of our history like a sinuous grey line. It was not until the nineteenth century, with the publication of Madame Bovary and the rise of materialism and of comfort in the home, that it fell out of favour; the fashion for the domestic novel helped to dethrone it, too. The taste for melodrama replaced it, and the monsters and other-worldly creatures were despised and half-forgotten.

But within ourselves, as a race, we went on desiring the story with 'the light that never was on land or sea', and presently, by devious ways, it began to creep back.

Of course, it had never quite vanished. It was merely hiding, which is what you would expect this kind of story to do. It looked out quite boldly in the *Alice* books, and in those of George MacDonald (a favourite author with Lewis, by the way) and right up through the final decades of the last century it can be found, usually out of print and lurking in volumes worn with reading and re-reading, in attic boxes, and on dusty shelves in the libraries of semi-private cultural institutions. H. G. Wells was a writer who began his literary career with this kind of book and, in my opinion, never wrote so well again after he had begun upon his more naturalistic works.

Some fifteen years ago the tale of the marvellous marched out, unheralded and confident, in the shape of science fiction.

Here she was, the right descendant of Grendel, with her lily-green complexion—the true colour of the Marvellous heroine—obscured by cosmetics from plastic containers and her silky hair, once free to the wind, teased into stiff shapes by the hairdresser. From her first free evening, too, the poor thing was dated by the superior critics, and has had to make her return into our affections handicapped by their approval and clinical interest.

Nevertheless, the return has been made and, in the right hands, she can appear what she truly is: Poetry's younger sister.

Lewis had those right hands. His three novels of science fiction, *That Hideous Strength*, *Perelandra*, and *Out of the Silent Planet*, hold all that we ask of this kind of story and they are also poetry; of a very old, pure, and satisfying kind, and packed with allegory and myth.

Perelandra is a sequel to *Out of the Silent Planet*, and the three books are linked by including the character Ransom (or Fisher-King—legend and allegory are often found in Lewis's use of names in the three stories) and by the central theme of dealings between our planet and others, out in what Lewis calls Deep Heaven. *That Hideous Strength*, while more exciting as pure narrative, is less poetic, more robustly human in treatment and in its recognition of the ordinary earthly meannesses and cowardices. And the bloody judgment at the end is raw Elizabethan bones-and-gristle stuff, a revelation of the force and violence of the writer's imagination.

But, indeed, Lewis had the right hands. How skilfully he introduced what may be called the 'stiffening' into these tales, the introduction of *invented fact*—in some cases, of actual fact—to give credibility to the incredible!

It may be doubted whether he was interested in machinery, and one can be certain that he did not consider descriptions of machines at work suitable to a work of poetic imagination. So he tells us about the vehicle in which Ransom travels between earth and the planets like this:

> The most noticeable thing in the room was the big white object. I recognized the shape well enough this time. It was a large coffin-shaped casket, open. On the floor beside it lay its lid and it was doubtless this that I had tripped over. Both were made of the same white material like ice, but more cloudy and less shining.

The ordinary reader can see it at once.

And in *Out of the Silent Planet* the accounts of the Sphere, in which the travellers go to Malacandra (or Mars) are even better:

> . . . all the walls looked as if they sloped outwards so as to make the room wider at the ceiling than at the floor, but each wall as you stood beside it turned out to be perfectly perpendicular—not only to sight but to touch also if one stooped down and examined with one's fingers the angle between it and the floor . . . the room was walled and floored with metal and was in a state of continuous faint vibration—a silent vibration with a strangely life-like and un-mechanical quality about it. But if the vibration was silent, there were plenty of noises going on—a series of musical raps or percussions at quite irregular intervals which seemed to come from the ceiling.

The sounds are made by the perpetual bombardment of tiny fragments of stars, hurtling past the machine.

'Exploiting the less observed properties of radiation' is how

Weston, one of the villains in the story, explains to Ransom the power which drives the Sphere, and the ordinary reader will be well-satisfied with a statement so authoritative.

Lewis, as a writer of imaginative fiction, had superb authority. It is one of the gifts usually overlooked in estimating a writer's work, and how the modern reader does unconsciously miss it, in nine contemporary novels out of ten!

The descriptions of Perelandra the planet itself can bear the word 'marvellous' in its full dictionary meaning—astonishing, extraordinary, preternatural—for what can be more astonishing than to imagine the soil and scents and noises on a speck of fire millions of miles from the Earth so vividly that the reader can actually feel a nostalgia for them, as if they had been personally experienced?

But even more marvellous are Lewis's accounts of the creatures that live on Malacandra.

In their creation, his gift soars until it touches the fringes of that region in Shakespeare's nature out of which the poet drew Ariel and Caliban, falling short only in that Shakespeare's fairy and monster are archtypes, Allfairy and Everymonster, and his supreme genius is shown in thus bodying forth images which exist—apparently—only in the mind of man.

Lewis's *sorns* and *hrossa* and *pfifltriggi* are not quite in this Olympus. But they dwell far up the sacred slope.

The stock figure of science fiction is what someone called, once and for always, the Bug-Eyed Monster. But the *sorns* and *hrossa* and other unknown creatures on Malacandra are monsters in Ransom's eyes only before he has met them, and Lewis cunningly first arouses the reader's imagination, then disturbs and frightens it, and lastly sets it furiously to work when he tells us Ransom's thoughts about them:

> But what was a *sorn*? 'When he saw them, he would eat out of Divine's hands.' His mind, like so many of his generation, was richly furnished with bogies. His universe was peopled

with horrors such as ancient and medieval mythology could hardly rival. No insect-like vermiculate or crustacean Abominable, no twitching feelers, rasping wings, slimy coils, curling tentacles, no monstrous union of superhuman intelligence and insatiable cruelty seemed to him anything but likely on an alien world. The *sorns* would be . . . would be . . . he dared not think what the *sorns* would be.

And then, when at last he is staying in a cave with a *sorn*—I use the rather social word *staying* deliberately, as if Lewis's hero were on a visit, which indeed he is—the *sorns* have their own humour—

> The *hrossa* should not have sent you this way. They do not seem to know from looking at an animal what sort of lungs it has and what it can do. It is just like a *hross*. If you had died on the *harandra* they would have made a poem about the gallant *hman* and how the sky grew black and the cold stars shone and he journeyed on and journeyed on and they would have put in a fine speech for you to say as you were dying . . . and all this would seem to them just as good as if they had used a little foresight and saved your life by sending you the easier way round.

and their own beauty—

> They seemed to Ransom to be skating rather than walking. The grace of their movement, their lofty stature and the softened glancing of the sunlight on their feathery sides effected a final transformation in Ransom's feelings towards their race. He had thought them spectral when they were only august, and his first human reaction to their lengthened severity of line and profound stillness of expression now appeared to him not so much cowardly as vulgar. So might Parmenides or Confucius look to the eyes of a Cockney schoolboy.

And—to continue my perhaps rather presumptuous comparisons of Lewis as an imaginative writer with writers of great genius—when I read the description of Ransom's journey on the *sorn's* back I recalled Dante's description of his ride on the back of the monster Geryon: in both accounts, physical contact with a creature from another world is imagined with astonishing vividness.

It is of course Reason which gives the *sorn* his acceptability; Reason, and humour. Lewis gives his creatures these two basically human characteristics, and then subtly modifies them by the use of elements widely differing from those experienced by Man. *Sorns* and *hrossa* can think and smile, but their thoughts and their smiles are not like human thoughts and smiles. His devils in *Perelandra* and *That Hideous Strength*—particularly in the latter book—are equally successful; indeed, Lewis himself described it as 'a tall story about devilry', and it recounts, as straightforwardly as any saga, the taking-over of a small university in England by a Ministry staffed by the creatures. The dialogue in this book is notably brilliant; each being talks as such a being would, and while the technique used in drawing them is broader than in either of the other two books, it fits the broader, more superficially sensational story.

If it be marvellous to create credible creatures in whom earthly blood does not run, even more marvellous is it to create pure Spirits, creatures outside the range of mankind's eyes and ears which do not live in a body made of bones and flesh at all. But Lewis succeeds with his *eldila* even as he succeeds with his *sorns* and *hrossa*.

This is how he strengthens our belief in them:

As a starting point for future investigation I recommend the following from Natvilcius (De Aethereo et aerio Corpore, Basel 1627 II xii); liquet simplicem flamman sensibus ... [and then Lewis gives us four lines of what is presumably seventeenth-century Latin and translates it for us] ... It appears that the homogeneous flame perceived by our senses is not the body properly so-called of an angel or daemon but rather either the sensorium or surface of that body or the surface of a body which exists after a manner beyond our conception in the celestial frame of spatial references . . . I take him to mean what we should now call 'multi-dimensional space', Lewis ends gently.

I, speaking as the common reader, do not know whether Natvilcius exists outside our author's imagination. But his name has a convincingly clumsy realness, like some of those names from the Ancient World that are so ugly you wonder how they came to be used as names—Odoacer, Soedeleube, Vaast—and I accept him without question. And when I want, also, to hear and realize the presence of an *eldil*, this is how Lewis lets me do it:

> The sound was quite astonishingly like a voice. It was perfectly articulate; it was even, I suppose, rather beautiful. But it was, if you understand me, inorganic. We feel the difference between animal voices (including those of the human animal) and all other noises pretty clearly, I fancy, though it is hard to define. Blood and lungs and the warm, moist cavity of the mouth are somehow indicated in every Voice. Here they were not. The two syllables sounded more as if they were played on an instrument than if they were spoken; yet they did not sound mechanical either. A machine is something we make out of natural materials; this was more as if rock crystal or light had spoken of itself.

Indeed, it is a strong imagination that can invent a sound for an imagined creature to make, and then brood upon that sound until it can bestow shades and variations in the voice of the creature it has created!

In *Perelandra*, most beautiful of the three science fiction books, and the most poetic, it seems to me at least that there is some quality preventing the picture from being entirely winning in Lewis's presentation of the Lady, the unfallen feminine spirit who cannot be called a woman but who gives us something of what, presumably, Lewis felt and thought about real women.

I fully realize that this is a delicate subject to write about when the writer never knew the author under discussion. But one does receive from this Portrait of another Lady an impression that Lewis disapproved of women.

I would not use a stronger word than 'disapproved', and I would qualify that by saying he disapproved of *some* women; women who have entered rather boldly into the world that men have reserved for themselves. The domesticated, fussy, kind, woman gets an occasional pat on her little head—(Mrs Beaver in *The Lion, the Witch and the Wardrobe*, Ivy Maggs in *That Hideous Strength*).

In *Perelandra* we see the Unman, or devil, working upon the Lady's weaknesses—or rather, putting weaknesses into her nature because she is capable of receiving them—and giving her what Lewis calls 'the dramatic conception of the self . . . making her mind a theatre in which that phantom self should hold the stage'.

He also (worse and worse—but then, he *is* a devil) gives her *a looking-glass*.

There is much of the 'crusty bachelor' in this attitude, and I even find it mildly endearing, but when Jane, the young wife in *That Hideous Strength*, is rebuked for trying to stick to her books and rather donnishly lectured for her lack of wifely obedience, I feel I must protest. Lewis's attitude is narrow and unkind.

So clever a man, with such a strong character, must have found childishness and silliness in women hard to put up with. But these faults (not entirely confined to one sex?) are not serious ones, and if women are not to walk boldly into the world of men nor to remain in their own world of foolish vanity, what are they to do? I am afraid Lewis implies that if they cannot be goddesses they are to go on suckling fools and chronicling small beer, and be disapproved of. There seems no way out of the situation and I prefer not to think any more about it.

The poet should be able to be fair to the flea. But it is a small, a very small, blot on Lewis's reputation as an *imaginative* writer.

The richness of these three science fiction novels is deep, and one regrets that Lewis himself did not think highly of them.

Apparently he did value his one 'straight' novel, *Till We Have Faces*, and was disappointed that it never gained much public favour.

Till We Have Faces is a difficult book, suggesting an Homeric or Icelandic saga written by Henry James, in less than Jamesian prose but with a Jamesian subtlety of psychology, and it needs a second, even a third, reading at short intervals if the impact of its beauty and force are to be fully felt.

It was called by Lewis 'this re-interpretation of an old story', which, he says, had haunted him since he was an undergraduate. The story is a very old one. It first appears in *The Golden Ass* of Apuleius, a writer born in the year 124, as a complete story inserted in the middle of a novel (a form that Dickens sometimes used) and since then it has wandered its way into countless romances and legends; Lewis is not the only writer to have been 'haunted' by it, and this is understandable, for it is an allegory of the human soul's love for God.

It has been suggested to me that in this story Lewis saw one of what he called 'good dreams' or 'those queer stories scattered all through heathen religions'; pre-Christian hints of the Christian relationship between Adam and his Creator. It is the story of Cupid and Psyche.

The tale in Lewis's version is told by an ugly princess, daughter of a king in a small barbarian kingdom. She has a marvellously beautiful younger sister named Istra—'in Greek it would be Psyche——', who is worshipped for her healing gifts and her beauty, as if she were indeed a goddess. When famine and war strike the kingdom, the heathen priest tells the king that Psyche must be sacrificed to the Brute, who lurks up in the mountains.

The ugly princess, Orual, goes up to the place of sacrifice to seek for her sister's bones. But instead she finds Psyche herself— joyous and as beautiful as ever, though sun-browned and in rags, and alive. Psyche, in long paragraphs full of the beautiful and perfectly weighted detail that Lewis knew so well how to write, tells her sister of her marriage with the God and ends by showing her his Palace, in which she now lives.

But Orual cannot see it. She can only see Psyche, happy in her rags, drinking brook water and calling it choice wine and eating wild berries and calling them 'food fit for the gods', and it seems clear to her that Psyche has become mad.

From this point, the story tells of the gradual discovery by Orual of the truth about herself, and bitter and sad it is, though full of pity.

Orual persuades her sister, by threatening to kill herself, to promise that she will take a lamp to look at her husband's face, using what is sometimes called 'emotional blackmail'.

In Psyche's speech to Orual, after the abortive suicide, there are echoes of the Lady's speeches in *Perelandra*.

'You are indeed teaching me about kinds of love that I did not know,' said Psyche. 'It is like looking into a deep pit. I am not sure whether I like your kind better than hatred. Oh Orual—to take my love for you, because you know it goes down to my very roots and cannot be diminished by any other, and then to make of it a tool, a weapon, and thing of policy and mastery, an instrument of torture . . . I begin to think I never knew you. Whatever comes after, something that was between us dies here.' 'Enough of your subtleties,' said I.

It cannot be denied that Lewis's view of Love was both high and severe. Between human beings, in its best form, he seems to have seen it as a form of charity, burningly strong and tempered by a detached intelligence and an unswerving watch upon itself to guard against the smallest taint of the usual heated, half-selfish, satisfyingly sloppy romanticism ever intruding.

Lewis asks much from human nature, and just occasionally in reading him, the mean sensual human heart shrinks. He is severe, as the good schoolmaster or the good priest is severe, and the common reader does not like severity. In *Till We Have Faces* the severity is apparent on every page, and I do think that it prevented the book from having a wide appeal.

The girl Orual is burdened so heavily, before she ever begins to deceive herself, by her ugliness. When she accuses the Gods of incomprehensibility, we feel that she has a strong case. Too much is asked of her.

Too much is asked of us all, perhaps. But it *is* asked and we have to do our best to give it. *Till We Have Faces* ends, however, with the dawn-flush without which it would be unbearable:

> She brought me now to the very edge of the pool. The air was growing brighter and brighter about us as if someone had set it on fire. Each breath I drew left me new terror, joy, overpowering sweetness. I loved (Psyche) as once I thought it would have been impossible to love . . . and yet it was not, not now, that she really counted. Or if she counted (and Oh, gloriously she did) it was for another's sake, and he was coming. The most dreadful, the most beautiful, the only dread and beauty there is, was coming . . . I cast down my eyes. Two figures, reflections, their feet to Psyche's feet and mine, stood head downwards in the water . . . Two Psyches, the one clothed, the other naked . . . both beautiful (as if that mattered now) beyond all imagining, yet not the same. 'You also are Psyche' came a great voice.

And Orual ends her story thus:

> I ended my first book with the words *no answer*. I know now, Lord, why you utter no answer. You are yourself the answer. Before your face questions die away.

A painful book; Lewis was not a writer to give adult people the easy happy ending. A blissful ending, yes, but that is another thing, and the ordinary reader does not ask for bliss, only a sweet taste on his palate at the end of the tale. A puzzling book, too: I feel that Lewis was clear about his allegories and symbols but I also feel that, like his Gods in the story, they do not make themselves clear.

On the strength of the character drawing in this book, I wish that Lewis could have written a 'straight' novel in a modern setting, but perhaps his mind, soaked since boyhood in saga and myth, could find no patience with modern people and their small dramas. He seems to have been perpetually haunted by the realities lying behind appearances; allegory was one of the deepest founts of his creative power.

Because he was so often severe, it is surprising to find humour and tenderness in his writing. The account of the bear, Mr Bultitude, in *That Hideous Strength*, is a serious attempt to tell us how a bear feels, but it is also endearing. And I am fond of the garden up at St Anne's-on-the-Hill:

> . . . like the garden in Peter Rabbit. Or was it like the garden in The Romance of the Rose? Not in the least like, really. Or like Klingsor's garden? Or the garden in Alice? Or like the garden on the top of some Mesopotamian ziggurat which had probably given rise to the whole legend of Paradise?

There is another quality in his writing, which is not fashionable today; cosiness.

Strange to find it side by side with severity. Yet there it is. It has left the modern novel; indeed, the word has become one of contempt. Lewis took no notice of fashion—if he had, he

G

would not have written a line—and all through the books there are firelight gleams of this despised and almost forgotten treat.

Tea, the embodiment of cosiness, is mentioned with telling effect in *Out of the Silent Planet*, while Ransom is awaiting his interview with the Oyarsa of Malacandra, the bodiless creature seemingly fashioned of light which governs the planet:

> He was thinking less of the invisible creature in the room [the messenger sent to summon him] than of the interview that lay before him. His old terrors of meeting some monster or idol had quite left him; he felt nervous as he remembered feeling on the morning of an examination when he was an undergraduate. More than anything in the world he would have liked a cup of good tea.

Again, beer is used to symbolize earthliness when Ransom returns to his own planet in the mysterious space-ship:

> There were voices from within and they were speaking English. There was a familiar smell. He pushed his way in, regardless of the surprise he was creating, and walked to the bar. 'A pint of bitter, please,' said Ransom.

Tea and beer! One thinks immediately of England.

And here I would like to say with diffidence that as an imaginative writer Lewis seems to me to be completely and satisfyingly English. He himself has told us of his boyhood entrancement by the sagas of Iceland, and in his work he must have read the books of almost every medieval writer in Europe, but while the impact of foreign culture may have widened a mind already wide enough to take in the conception of Deep Heaven, it did not affect his native bluntness and fresh poetry.

These qualities come out forthrightly—as if, with a sigh of pleasure, all the brakes had been taken off—in his seven books for children, the Narnia stories.

All the things that he seems to have liked best are here:

magic, talking animals, a group of friends having adventures, the over-riding moral sense, danger and courage in face of it, and, of course, allegory.

In the first story, *The Lion, the Witch and the Wardrobe*, *tea* makes another of those comforting appearances, and there is a typically Lewisian picture of Father Christmas:

> Everybody knew him, because, though you see people of his sort only in Narnia, you see pictures of them and hear them talked about even in our world, the world on this side of a wardrobe door. But when you really see them in Narnia it is rather different. Some of the pictures of Father Christmas in our world make him look only funny and jolly. But now that the children actually stood looking at him they didn't find it quite like that. He was so big, and so glad, that they all became quite still. They felt very glad but also solemn.

The children have entered Narnia through the door of a wardrobe filled with old coats, and Father Christmas has come as part of the breaking of a spell put on the land by the Witch, the land 'where it is always winter but Christmas never comes' (and here the allegory rings faintly in the reader's mind like long-ago Christmas chimes). After giving the three children and Mr and Mrs Beaver suitable presents, 'he suddenly looked less grave'.

> '. . . here is something for you all!' and he brought out (I suppose from the big bag at his back but nobody saw him do it) a large tray containing five cups and saucers, a bowl of lump sugar, a jug of cream, and a great big tea-pot, all sizzling and piping hot. Then he cried out 'Merry Christmas! Long live the true King!', and he and the reindeer and the sledge were out of sight before anyone realized they had started.

Mrs Beaver says it was a mercy she thought of bringing the bread knife—I imagine Mrs Beaver stands for the practical, sensible spirit in women which Lewis approved—and all five return to the cave in which they are hiding from the Witch's wicked wolf-police and 'Mr Beaver cut some of the bread and ham into sandwiches and Mrs Beaver poured out the tea and everyone enjoyed themselves'—including the adult reader, an almost forgotten experience for the poor soul.

In the following Narnia books the allegory is much stronger and more plain, so strong that when, in *The Last Battle*, the final book of the series, I found the great lion who has haunted the former stories given a capital H—'and as He spoke He no longer looked to them like a lion'—I felt a shock: not, of course, with any implication of disapproval, but pure shock, as if cold water had spouted up from the page.

Hints of what was to come are given in the earlier books, as when the Lion dies—and returns to life again—in order to save the boy Edmund, who has acted the part of a traitor.

Most of us modern Christians are poor weak creatures, and tend to be over-conscious of two thousand years being a very long time; even if we have not been trained in scientific thinking we have unconsciously absorbed some of the half-baked and one-sided thinking that floats uneasily around in this most unhappy age, and we tend to see Christ as pictured and static and *past*. I do not believe that Lewis was thus hampered. I believe that his reading in medieval literature and his painfully-acquired faith conspired to give him a personal feeling for Christ and an intellectual conception of His immediacy that was exceedingly strong; it would be a commonplace, to Lewis, to conceive of Christ under the likeness of a Lion, a Lamb, a Fish. In the interplanetary stories he dares to give Him another name—*Maledil*. (One is reminded of Alice Meynell's poem *Christ in the Universe*.)

Thinking it out, I was no longer shocked by the symbol of Christ as a mighty golden Lion, combining majesty and tender fatherly comfort. It is a child's picture, this dazzling golden heraldic Beast on fire with Divine Love that yet can be nestled up to, and perhaps the true shock comes from picturing the contrast between the enormous creature's power, and its gentleness when it calls the child 'dear heart'.

This is very bold. Its boldness makes that of some contemporary writers look inept.

Yet I confess that I do not altogether *like* it, and it could be argued that the tremendousness of the allegory mars the artistry of the tale.

I imagine the accusation would pass Lewis by completely. He would not have thought that it mattered.

Mr Leavis, the critic, has rebuked readers and other critics for crediting writers with possessing genius because they can 'make a world', and none of us like to be rebuked. Still, I feel that we shall continue to credit writers thus, and perhaps we may remind our mentor that it is not every writer who *can* create a world.

C. S. Lewis did, a beautiful and dangerous world lit by hope. I suppose that in his imaginative writing he might be accused of ignoring the travails and discoveries and ethos of the contemporary scene. In my opinion at least, it is all, as an imaginative writer, that he can be accused of.

6

From a Poet

BY

KATHLEEN RAINE

I KNEW C. S. LEWIS only during his last years when he was
Professor of English at Cambridge. His arrival there coincided
with my own, it so happened; I had been invited to return to
my old College (Girton) as a Research Fellow, in order to
complete my work on William Blake. This invitation came
through Dr Bradbrook, who had herself been a pupil of C. S.
Lewis for a time in Oxford, and it was she who invited him
out to Girton to the dinner-party at which I met him for the
first time. I had not expected to like him so much, for at that
time I had read only *The Problem of Pain* and *The Screwtape
Letters* which I did not feel to be in any way for me; but to
meet him was to know that here was a man of great learning,
continuously kindled into life by imagination. He seemed to
possess a kind of boyish greatness—an unique combination of
qualities, in my experience, for in him neither seemed to vitiate
the other. He was not, certainly intellectually boyish (no reader
of his works of scholarship could suppose that) but in the freshness and joyousness with which he carried his learning. I think
of Stevenson's line as particularly applicable to him, 'Glory of
youth glowed in his soul.' The sense of glory has become rare,
even in youth; was it perhaps an Irish trait in him, never to

doubt the worth of the game?—and for him learning was a joyful and inexhaustible game.

Among so many academic figures whose attitude towards literature was one of bored superiority or active hatred, his love of the material itself was life-giving as a spring in a desert. I went to some of his lectures on the 'matter' of Rome, France, and Britain, and remember how he made the dullest Latin text seem enthralling (he would I am sure here have retorted that no one could possibly consider Boethius dull). The element of play was never far away. He came to tea one day I remember, and walking in the Girton grounds began to imagine how Dryden would have written Blake's *The Tyger*. He produced instantly a fine couplet (I wish I could remember it) then exclaimed, 'No, that is much too good for Dryden, it is almost good enough for Pope,' and unhesitatingly set about polishing it up to Pope's standard. He could put together clear well-made sentences even in verse, and I have heard him express astonishment at how badly a certain world-famous professional colleague put together even the simplest sentence—a sign, he thought, of a fundamental insensitivity to language.

He took a poor view of 'literary criticism' and once asked me if I did not think it entirely useless? I said that I did: scholarship can help towards the better understanding of a poem whose difficulty arises from our lack of certain knowledge; but criticism is a kind of mould or cancer. I found in him an enthusiastic ally in my own work on the sources of William Blake, and little more than a week before his death I received a letter from him from which, since its application goes beyond my own work, I quote: 'Yes. Once one goes in for Blake (or Milton or Kipling) one meets, disguised as literary critics, a great many dissentients of quite a different sort. But you'll knock 'em all down, like a second Camilla. Plenty of fact, reasoning as brief and clear as English sunshine, and no personal comment at all.' That was the only kind of criticism he saw any use for.

He wrote, I imagine, many of these charming encouraging letters, for he was generous and valued the good for its own sake and not for personal motives. His advice to me describes very well his own practice. On one occasion William Empson came to deliver a lecture on *Paradise Lost* to the Modern Languages Society. The occasion was a distinguished one, in the beautiful long gallery of Emmanuel. Professors Willey and Tillyard were also present among the élite there assembled. William Empson gave a brilliant and perverse performance; his paper contained many provocative anti-Christian asides which one might have expected Professor Lewis to take up. He did not; he took William Empson up solely (and very thoroughly) on matters of text, reducing him in a shorter time than it took Socrates to deal with Thrasymachus, to a condition of extreme mildness—he too, it is but just to say, respecting the rules of the game.

The complete absence in him of academic envy may have come from the artist in him, happily fulfilled surely in his children's books. I have given away many sets of these to children, who accept Narnia with a passion that testifies to its truth to some world of imagination we all share. I delight in them myself, and never find that they pall in however many readings children may demand.

When he was already seriously ill I visited him occasionally in his rooms in Magdalene. He would make a bachelor pot of tea (he was then in fact a widower) and the talk was as fresh as ever; never personal. He thought of me as an incorrigible Platonist, but in private life he did not proselytize or persuade. I remember conversation with him as delightful because even though at the full extent of my own learning, beyond (and even within) the narrow field in which I had been working he was more than a match for me; every conversation was an exploration, or a game with a shining ball flying through the air.

What was best of all in his immense learning was that it had an orientation; almost—not quite—alone in the Cambridge of that time he understood that poetry and the other arts are the language of tradition, and exist to serve ends which are not literary. Doubtless he would have agreed with Dom Bede Griffiths (another of his old students) that the function of art is 'to evoke the divine presence'. One cannot take seriously— one cannot even play at (or should I say least of all can one play at)—literary discussion with those who believe less.

7

Impact on America

BY

CHAD WALSH

To WRITE about Lewis's impact on America is a presumptuous undertaking for any lone individual. If I were to do it in good American fashion I suppose I should approach one of the great philanthropic organizations and ask for an adequate grant and a staff of social scientists to accomplish the field work for me. We should then send out vast numbers of questionnaires and dispatch a crew of interviewers to question a sufficient cross-section of the population. Certainly, Lewis's impact was both broad and deep and it undoubtedly reached more sorts and conditions of men than I can enumerate from personal observation.

Short of a grand scale sociological enterprise of this kind, the best I can do is to set down in all candour my own personal impressions based on hit-or-miss witness during the twenty years that elapsed between the American publication of *The Screwtape Letters* in 1943 and the death of C. S. Lewis on the same date that saw the assassination of President Kennedy. During those two decades I am convinced that he had an impact on American religious thinking and indeed on the American religious imagination which has been very rarely, if ever, equalled by any other modern writer.

The reputation of Lewis spread pre-eminently by word of mouth. My own experience was typical. It was around 1944 or 1945 when I was taking a brief vacation from my wartime job and was visiting in Middlebury, Vermont. There I happened one day to be talking with my good friend, Dr Viola White, who was curator of the Americana section of the Middlebury College Library. A devout Episcopalian as well as lover of literature, she told me in great excitement about a book she had just read called *Perelandra*. Such was her missionary spirit that she lent it to me and I started reading it. I quickly consumed it from cover to cover. I was struck first of all by the sheer beauty of the book. It transported me into a kind of Elysian Fields—or better yet, an unspoiled Eden, inhabited by the innocent and unfallen. The second thing that struck me was that here at last was science fiction as science fiction at its fullest development should be. I had long been a devotee of the little green men on Mars with their tentacles and extra ears, and long before the launching of the first Sputnik I had been convinced that interplanetary communication would become possible. But it had seemed to me that science fiction was being used mostly for trivial purposes whereas it could be the vehicle of great philosophic and psychological myth. Here was Lewis, about whom I knew almost nothing, proving the truth of my stubborn conviction. Finally, and most importantly, in *Perelandra* I found my imagination being baptized. At the time I was slowly thinking, feeling, and fumbling my way towards the Christian faith and had reached the point where I was more than half convinced that it was true. This conviction, however, was a thing more of the mind than of the imagination and heart. In *Perelandra* I got the taste and the smell of Christian truth. My senses as well as my soul were baptized. It was as though an intellectual abstraction or speculation had become flesh and dwelt in its solid bodily glory among us.

I have narrated my true confessions at some length, not

because they are important but because they are typical. A friend came on a book of Lewis's and took delight in it. She lent it to me. The result was that I began buying everything else by him that was available in America and also passed along word of the discovery to other friends. It was as though I had discovered a new ingredient in my intellectual, emotional, and spiritual diet that I had unconsciously desired but had not previously found. I think many others, coming on Lewis for the first time, felt the same way.

It was three or four years later that I felt moved to go to England and gather material for the first book on C. S. Lewis.[1] By that time Lewis had become almost an American institution. But his standing in America involved certain subtle and some not so subtle distinctions as compared with his standing in England. In the first place, in England he had gradually established a substantial scholarly reputation in the field of literature during the 1930s. A few specialists in America were also familiar with his work, but undoubtedly he was better known in his home country. When he began turning his primary attention to Christian apologetics there was an impressive number of English scholars who regarded with apprehension and disapproval his shift of emphasis. In 1948, during my visit to England, it was very easy to detect this attitude— 'Poor Lewis, I wish he would return to his last. Why does he insist upon going into areas that he really doesn't know anything about?' To most of the specialists in literature he seemed a prime example of a man who was at the point where he could have crowned his academic career with some work of supreme importance but chose instead to become a literary evangelist writing for the educationally unwashed as well as the elite. Nor were the British theologians unanimous in their welcome. I detected more than one twinge of professional envy as I

[1] *C. S. Lewis: Apostle to the Skeptics*, The Macmillan Company, New York. Now out of print.

talked with some of them. Who, they seemed to be asking, is this upstart who has not had the benefit of formal theological training or the laying on of hands and who yet presumes to preach the gospel to a vaster audience than we can reach? Some also felt that he was a regrettable simplifier who presented the gospel in an overly digestible form to an uncritical public.

In America, by contrast, Lewis's wide reputation began all at once in 1943 when the American edition of *The Screwtape Letters* was published. The combination of urbanity, wit, imagination and uncompromising orthodoxy caught the imagination of many reviewers and a large reading public. 'Whatever you may think of the theses of Mr Lewis' (Leonard Bacon wrote in his review of *The Screwtape Letters*), 'presented as they are in a bizarre and slantindicular manner, the fact remains that there is a spectacular and satisfactory nova in the bleak sky of satire.' It had been a long time (perhaps G. K. Chesterton was the last) since this combination of passionate faith and wit had been available. And it contrasted mightily with the dull or heavily strident works of most religious writers. A certain snob quality may have entered into the appeal of *The Screwtape Letters*. Here at last was a religious book, indeed a specifically Christian book, written with such sophistication and elegance that one need not apologize for leaving it out on the coffee table.

There was, of course, more to *The Screwtape Letters* than intellectual brilliance and a slight appeal to intellectual snobbery. The book was and remains a masterpiece of psychological understanding. Many a reader who came on it in one fashion or another recognized himself in the young Christian convert who is the central character—one scarcely dares say hero—of the book. The routine and undramatic temptations of daily life are brilliantly depicted and analysed by the infernal Screwtape. In short, it was a book that rang true to actual human experience and as such it seems destined for a very long life indeed.

The Screwtape Letters established Lewis's beachhead in America, which was quickly expanded as his older books were brought out in American editions and new works poured from his fruitful pen, to be simultaneously published on both sides of the Atlantic. His appeal, as I hope to show shortly, was a multiple one. He touched different intellectual levels and different casts of minds. Undoubtedly one factor and perhaps a major one was his status as an 'amateur'. America has never been very much given to anti-clericalism in the European sense, but there is an ancient and widespread American tradition of regarding the clergy and theologians as being up in the clouds and not saying anything too relevant to the earth as it actually exists. Lewis's credentials were that he had solidly established himself in a field which most people might not understand but at least vaguely respected. With this base he was able to venture forth into theology and gain a more respectful hearing with many readers than would have been possible if he had been a seminary professor. There was also the feeling that he had no vested interest in religion. His bread and butter did not depend upon it. Thus a great many persons who brought an attitude of suspicion to bear upon the outpourings of professionals were willing to listen to him.

Certainly, he quickly gained a wide audience. I suppose, speaking in terms of 'brows' rather than classes, it was predominately high-brow and middle-brow, though I cannot be dogmatic about this. I suspect that some people of quite humble educational and intellectual backgrounds also found much meat in his writing. I have already mentioned his appeal to the intellectuals. This was especially strong in the case of those who had a strong literary or humanistic bias. They intuitively recognized him as one of themselves—not only because of his professional area of specialization, but because of the civilized way he wrote. His mind also operated in a way easy for the humanistic sensibility to follow. I am quite sure that his appeal to those whose orientation was primarily scientific was much less but not totally lacking. The 'two cultures' exist in America as well as in England though the lines of demarcation are not as sharp. It is also a common phenomenon for the American scientist to keep his science in one lobe of his brain and his religion in the other. This made it possible for some scientific readers to disregard Lewis's lack of scientific background and orientation and to appreciate him simply as a religious writer.

Certainly Lewis performed a special mission with people who were slowly finding their way towards some sort of Christian orthodoxy. The background of such a person might vary greatly. Some had been brought up in super-orthodox churches—frequently of a very puritanical sort—and had revolted violently against their heritage.[1] Later on they perhaps came to a point where they reconsidered Christianity and they frequently passed through various stages of liberal protestantism while groping their way towards historic Christianity. Others had no religious background to speak of. America now has a fair number of second and third generation agnostics. What these various readers had in common was a desire for a religious faith which would have its roots sunk deep in the main Christian tradition but which would not do violence, to their intellects and knowledge. They wanted 'orthodoxy', not 'an obscurantist fundamentalism'. They found what they were looking for in Lewis. If one were able to do a survey of the type I wryly suggested earlier, I think an astonishing number of persons could be discovered whose way of looking at Christianity and whose categories of religious thought come straight out of the pages of C. S. Lewis.

[1] The outright 'Fundamentalists' also welcomed Lewis as an ally, though many regretted that he was not specific enough about the inerrancy of the Scriptures.

He had, surprisingly or perhaps not surprisingly, a large following among Roman Catholics. This was borne in upon me many years ago when I was at Marquette University—an excellent Jesuit institution in Milwaukee, Wisconsin—to take part in a symposium. I was talking with a number of professors there, all of whom were Roman Catholics. I kept leading the conversation around to Evelyn Waugh and Graham Greene. They kept leading it back to C. S. Lewis and Charles Williams. Though any Roman Catholic would wish that Lewis had gone farther at a number of points they seem to find little to criticize in what he said as far as he went. They also find in him a fresh and vital restatement of the doctrines that they learned more drily in Catechism.

Lewis was lucky in his timing. He first came to general American attention in the middle of the Second World War. During the 1930s America had been so preoccupied with its social and economic problems that there was relatively little interest in religion. Men were too busy trying to do something about the bread lines, the soup kitchens, economic stagnation, and the problems of labour relationships to have much time and energy for theological matters. It is significant that the most esteemed American theologian of that period was Reinhold Neibuhr with his very strong economic and political emphasis.

During the course of the Second World War the atmosphere gradually changed. Perhaps a war, bringing suffering and widespread death, always encourages a reopening of the ancient questions with which religion deals. Whatever the reason there was a marked increase in the percentage of people concerned about religion and indeed actively involved in churches. Soon many publishing houses that had brought out only an occasional religious book were setting up special departments. Religion was in the air. On all social and educational levels (from the crudest revivalist to the most rarefied theologian) it was much more talked about than it had been for some time. Looking back now after the wave has somewhat subsided, it is difficult to say how much was genuine and how much was verbal. At any rate, religion was in the public eye to a greater extent than it had been previously and more than it is today. I should say that this period, which began during the Second World War, extended at least into the middle or late 1950s, and that it coincided with the time when the enthusiasm for C. S. Lewis was most evident in America.

Several times I have suggested that Lewis had an appeal which cut across many lines of class and education. It remains true, however, that he had an especially strong following in the academic world. I suspect this was even more true in America than in England. At any rate, America boasts the distinction that at least five doctoral dissertations dealing with various aspects of Lewis's work have been duly written and submitted.[1] Lewis himself always did his best to discourage such works of scholarship. When I first broke the news to him that I was planning to write a book about him he besought me to wait until he was safely dead. It may be, of course, that the output of dissertations in America reflects a difference in attitude towards the Ph.D. rather than a markedly stronger interest in Lewis on the part of academic people in the United States.

On the whole Lewis fared well in America from the professional theologians. Though many of them must have felt that he stated things too simply and almost too clearly they were glad to have such a gifted ally in the war against secularist thought. His works were particularly popular with clergy who were on the intellectual firing line—for example, college and university chaplains. It sometimes seemed that they bought his books by the gross in order to give them to eager young intellectuals who were disturbed by religious questions.

[1] Discussed in Clyde S. Kilby, *The Christian World of C. S. Lewis.*

H

Not, of course, that Lewis escaped scotfree from severe criticism. Many of the philosophers gunned for him, and T. V. Smith, in his review of *Miracles*, was gentler than many when he exclaimed: 'At the ingenuity of this book I stand aghast. But I am not touched by its covert appeal to piety, nor moved to credence by its overt argument. It is modernistic apologetics for Christian fundamentalism.' The most notable attack by the theologians was that launched by the Reverend Professor W. Norman Pittenger, of General Theological Seminary (New York). In an article entitled 'Apologist versus Apologist' (*The Christian Century*, 1 October 1958) he berated Lewis as an oversimplifer, and fastened several labels of heresy upon him: 'Mr Lewis's Christology, his doctrine of Christ, is outright Docetic, even Gnostic.' Lewis, with a barbed meekness, published a reply in which he said that if the professional theologians had been able to make contact with the general public, it would not be necessary for such inept amateurs as himself to do the job.

Even at his heyday Lewis's books did not appeal to everyone. Some people, and these were often highly intelligent but rather flatminded souls, considered him a 'smart aleck'. They did not take kindly to his wit and his paradoxes. They felt that he was being clever with serious things. In my dealings with college students I discovered that either his books would speak immediately to the condition of a given student or it would scarcely speak at all. There was seldom an intermediate reaction. Some readers also found him over-rationalistic or over-moralistic. They felt that he was stronger on the fact of law than the mystery of grace. These readers were frequently people who turned more readily to Charles Williams and found in him a depth that they considered missing from the Oxford don.

I have suggested that Lewis's influence for the time being has somewhat declined in America. I think the main reason is the waning of the great religious trend that prevailed from the Second World War for at least a decade afterwards. This trend has slowly reversed. Or perhaps it would be better to say that it has taken different forms. Among college students I hear much less talk about religion than ten years ago. They are not inclined to argue about either its truth or falsity. They are much more concerned, when they think of it at all, with its relevance. The most profound expression of religious feeling among young people in America today is probably member-ship in the Peace Corps or participation in inter-racial activities and demonstrations. It is action rather than talk and theorizing. To such young persons Lewis seems much too theoretical and abstract. They find in his books very little having to do with political and social questions and it is these dilemmas that dominate the thought and feeling of the more perceptive young people in America today. I think they also find him too much of a rationalist and Thomist for their tastes. The in-tellectual climate in America is increasingly dominated by a kind of diffused existentialism. It is not that most people, whether university students or not, have read the works of the existentialists, but rather that an existentialist stance has some-how come into being. Lewis's schematic works do not fit well with the existentialists' toe-hold in the universe.

This interim report would therefore have to admit that Lewis's influence for the moment is on the wane in America. This is not to deny that many of his books continue to sell well. It is simply that he is less talked about than ten or fifteen years ago. I suppose that he is entering into a period of relative obscurity; future decades will determine what his final standing in America is. This happens with almost every writer sooner or later. My own prediction, for what it is worth, is that his straightforward books, such as *Broadcast Talks*, will not last forever. They were splendid religious journalism, but each age should produce its own journalists. I am, however, equally convinced that his more imaginative books will live on with full force and become a permanent part of the literary and religious heritage. I am thinking, for example, of *The Screwtape Letters* (his most popular book in America) *The Great Divorce*, the three interplanetary novels, and that superb series of seven Narnia novels for children. In these books where his imagination has full scope he presents the Christian faith in a more eloquent and probing way than ever his more straightforward books of apologetics could. These books are not for a day but for a very long time to come.

One other thing should be said about Lewis's impact on America. Only after as many of his letters as possible have been collected will it be possible to know how many Americans corresponded with him occasionally or on a more-or-less regular basis. I think it will be discovered that an astonishing number did, and that Lewis was extraordinarily generous of his time and attention. I know many individuals who wrote to him, not merely about theological matters but about their own deep-seated personal and religious problems. I have seen some of the letters he wrote in reply. Any consideration of his impact on America must take these letters into account. Though no bishop ever laid hands upon his head, he was a genuine pastoral counsellor via the postal system to many fellow pilgrims who perhaps never sat in the study of an ordained minister.

It is very hard to realize that he is no more with us. Like many other Americans I made the pilgrimage to that rambling brick house in Kiln Lane. I had the privilege of knowing him personally as well as admiring from afar. One may see certain blind spots in his books, but as a human being he was a whole man and a loveable one. I am also convinced that in his books at their best, there was a radiant and utterly real quality hard to find in other twentieth-century writings, and that half a dozen at least of his books will take their place among the classics of religious literature.

8

A Bibliography of the Writings
of C. S. Lewis

BY

WALTER HOOPER

IF IT could talk, C. S. Lewis's waste-paper basket might tell the perfect bibliographical story. Lewis tossed almost every copy of his own books, and all his contributions to periodicals, in the 'W.P.B.' as he called it. And just as promptly forgot what he had written.

When I became his secretary, I had already compiled an enormous collection of his writings. I showed Lewis my bibliography, which surprised him. 'Did *I* write all these?' he asked, and thereafter named me his Pseudo-Dionysius on the grounds that I had invented most of them. But I could never change his habit of dealing with his own works. One day, on entering the sitting-room, I discovered him dumping *my* copies of his books into the waste-paper basket. Even though I suspect that Lewis was gratified, my collector's habit continued a standing joke between us. So much so, that during one of his last illnesses, as I was taking the tea tray out, he said, shaking his finger, 'I know what the divine joke on you would be. One day, as soon as the door is closed behind you, I will utter my last immortal words and *you* shan't get to hear them!' I remember suggesting that he keep a pencil and pad close by.

And yet Lewis had a marvellous memory. Following his retirement from Cambridge, he sent me to Magdalene College with seven pages of instructions about the care and disposal of every book in his library. The only order respecting his own works was 'All my own books W.P.B. or apply to your own use.' Needless to say, the W.P.B. went empty.

I cannot claim that this bibliography is by any means definitive even though it has been the work of many years and includes everything that I have been able to find. Nevertheless, it seems important to establish, as it were, something of a Lewis 'canon' so that it can be known what 'Lewisiana' has been collected. Apart from the works Lewis wrote during the time I was with him, he never remembered, for the purposes of this project, a single item. My usual method was to sit down in the Bodleian with bound issues of, say, *The Oxford Magazine*, and search each page from 1917 onwards.

And yet . . . much as I hang on every word that Lewis wrote, I would happily exchange all for one more conversation with him over tea in the sitting-room of the Kilns. But content we must all remain with the huge legacy he has left us.

Among my numerous debts I owe especial thanks to Lewis's foster-sister, Lady Dunbar of Hempriggs, and Mr Leonard Blake. I am also grateful to Dr R. W. Ladborough, Mr Owen Barfield, Dr and Mrs Austin Farrer, Mr Roger Lancelyn Green, Professor Chad Walsh, Dr Lawrence F. London, and Mrs Juanita Jackson for helping me find many of the items listed below. Mr G. G. Barber of the Bodleian Library and Mr Peter Meade of the British Museum gave me valuable assistance in the arrangement of my material. And last, for his many kindnesses, I thank my friend, Major W. H. Lewis.

A NOTE ON THE USE OF THE BIBLIOGRAPHY

This bibliography is divided into seven sections in which the items are arranged and numbered chronologically. They are

A: Books
B: Short Stories
C: Books edited or with Prefaces by C. S. Lewis
D: Essays and Pamphlets
E: Poems
F: Book reviews by C. S. Lewis
G: Published Letters

The Index, which follows, is designed to help locate items by title. For instance, *Perelandra*, a book in Section A, is numbered 13. Thus, in the Index one finds the combination, *Perelandra*, A13. The same method is used throughout except for 'Books reviewed' and 'Published Letters' which are grouped separately.

One will also find some cross-references. For example, 'The Personal Heresy in Criticism' (D5) was originally published as an essay. Later it became the first chapter of *The Personal Heresy* (A7). Consequently, in the Index one finds the entry, *Personal Heresy in Criticism, The*, D5, A7. However, the converse is not the same; D5 is *part* of A7, but A7 is *not* part of D5.

This bibliography includes only the original issues of Lewis's published writings as well as their re-appearance in collections of his own essays and poems. In every case I have given the full title of each piece in expectation that the bibliography may be useful to librarians and scholars.

I should mention that *The Guardian* (1846–1951) in which *The Screwtape Letters* originally appeared was a religious newspaper, now out of print, and not to be confused with *The Guardian* (formerly, *The Manchester Guardian*) in print today.

The *Cherbourg School Magazine*, the rarest item on my bibliography, was published by Cherbourg School, Malvern, Worcestershire, when Lewis was a pupil there. It is, in fact, the same school which he calls 'Chartres' in *Surprised by Joy*. It has since become a girls' school, Ellerslie.

A BIBLIOGRAPHY OF THE WRITINGS OF C. S. LEWIS

A Books

1 *Spirits in Bondage: A Cycle of Lyrics* London: William Heinemann Ltd, 1919 (under the pseudonym of Clive Hamilton)

2 *Dymer* London: J. M. Dent and Sons, 1926 (under the pseudonym of Clive Hamilton); reprinted with a new Preface, as by C. S. Lewis, 1950

3 *The Pilgrim's Regress: An Allegorical Apology for Christianity, Reason and Romanticism* London: J. M. Dent and Sons, 1933; London: Sheed and Ward, 1935; London: Geoffrey Bles Ltd, 1943, with the author's important new Preface on Romanticism, footnotes, and running headlines

4 *The Allegory of Love: A Study in Medieval Tradition* Oxford: Clarendon Press, 1936; reprinted with corrections, London: Oxford University Press, 1938

5 *Out of the Silent Planet* London: John Lane, 1938

6 *Rehabilitations and Other Essays* London, New York, Toronto: Oxford University Press, 1939. (Contents: 'Shelley, Dryden, and Mr Eliot', 'William Morris', 'The Idea of an "English School"', 'Our English Syllabus', 'High and Low Brows', 'The Alliterative Metre', 'Bluspels and Flalansferes: A Semantic Nightmare', 'Variation in Shakespeare and Others', 'Christianity and Literature')

7 (With E. M. W. Tillyard) *The Personal Heresy: A Controversy* London, New York, Toronto: Oxford University Press, 1939

8 *The Problem of Pain* London: Geoffrey Bles Ltd, 1940

9 *The Screwtape Letters* London: Geoffrey Bles Ltd, 1942; reprinted with a new Screwtape letter as *The Screwtape Letters and Screwtape Proposes a Toast*, with a new and additional Preface, 1961

10 *A Preface to 'Paradise Lost': Being the Ballard Matthews Lectures Delivered at University College, North Wales, 1941, Revised and Enlarged* London, New York, Toronto: Oxford University Press, 1942

11 *Broadcast Talks: Reprinted with Some Alterations from Two Series of Broadcast Talks ('Right and Wrong: A Clue to the Meaning of the Universe' and 'What Christians Believe') Given in 1941 and 1942* London: Geoffrey Bles Ltd, 1942

12 *Christian Behaviour: A Further Series of Broadcast Talks* London: Geoffrey Bles Ltd, 1943

13 *Perelandra* London: John Lane, 1943. Also published as *Voyage to Venus*, London: Pan Books Ltd, 1953

14 *The Abolition of Man, or, Reflections on Education with Special Reference to the Teaching of English in the Upper Forms of Schools* Riddell Memorial Lectures, Fifteenth Series. London: Oxford University Press, 1943; London: Geoffrey Bles Ltd, 1946

15 *Beyond Personality: The Christian Idea of God* London: Geoffrey Bles Ltd, 1944

16 *That Hideous Strength: A Modern Fairy-Tale for Grown-ups* London: John Lane, 1945. Also published in an abridged form, with a different Preface, as *That Hideous Strength*, London: Pan Books Ltd, 1955

17 *The Great Divorce: A Dream* London: Geoffrey Bles Ltd, 1946

18 *Miracles: A Preliminary Study* London: Geoffrey Bles Ltd, 1947. With revision of Chapter III, London: Fontana Books, 1960

19 *Transposition and Other Addresses* London: Geoffrey Bles Ltd, 1949. (Contents: 'Transposition', 'The Weight of Glory', 'Membership', 'Learning in War-Time', 'The Inner Ring')

20 *The Lion, the Witch and the Wardrobe* Illustrated by Pauline Baynes. London: Geoffrey Bles Ltd, 1950

21 *Prince Caspian: The Return to Narnia* Illustrated by Pauline Baynes. London: Geoffrey Bles Ltd, 1951

22 *Mere Christianity: A Revised and Amplified Edition, with a New Introduction, of the Three Books 'Broadcast Talks', 'Christian Behaviour', and 'Beyond Personality'* London: Geoffrey Bles Ltd, 1952

23 *The Voyage of the 'Dawn Treader'* Illustrated by Pauline Baynes. London: Geoffrey Bles Ltd, 1952

24 *The Silver Chair* Illustrated by Pauline Baynes. London: Geoffrey Bles Ltd, 1953

25 *The Horse and His Boy* Illustrated by Pauline Baynes. London: Geoffrey Bles Ltd, 1954

26 *English Literature in the Sixteenth Century, excluding Drama* The Completion of 'The Clark Lectures', Trinity College, Cambridge, 1944 (*The Oxford History of English Literature*, Vol. III). Oxford: Clarendon Press, 1954

27 *The Magician's Nephew* Illustrated by Pauline Baynes. London: The Bodley Head, 1955

28 *Surprised by Joy: The Shape of My Early Life* London: Geoffrey Bles Ltd, 1955

29 *The Last Battle* Illustrated by Pauline Baynes. London: The Bodley Head, 1956

30 *Till We Have Faces: A Myth Retold* London: Geoffrey Bles Ltd, 1956

31 *Reflections on the Psalms* London: Geoffrey Bles Ltd, 1958

32 *The Four Loves* London: Geoffrey Bles Ltd, 1960

33 *Studies in Words* Cambridge: Cambridge University Press, 1960

34 *The World's Last Night and Other Essays* New York: Harcourt, Brace and Co., 1960. (Contents: 'The Efficacy of Prayer', 'On Obstinacy in Belief', 'Lilies that Fester', 'Screwtape Proposes a Toast', 'Good Work and Good Works', 'Religion and Rocketry', 'The World's Last Night')

35 *A Grief Observed* London: Faber and Faber, 1961 (under the pseudonym of N. W. Clerk); reprinted, as by C. S. Lewis, 1964

36 *An Experiment in Criticism* Cambridge: Cambridge University Press, 1961

37 *They Asked for a Paper: Papers and Addresses* London: Geoffrey Bles Ltd, 1962. (Contents: '*De Descriptione Temporum*', 'The Literary Impact of the Authorised Version', 'Hamlet: The Prince or the Poem?', 'Kipling's World', 'Sir Walter Scott', 'Lilies that Fester', 'Psycho-analysis and Literary Criticism', 'The Inner Ring', 'Is Theology Poetry?', 'Transposition', 'On Obstinacy in Belief', 'The Weight of Glory')

38 *Beyond the Bright Blur* New York: Harcourt, Brace and World, Inc., 1963. (On the flyleaf: '*Beyond the Bright Blur* is taken from *Letters to Malcolm: Chiefly on Prayer* [Chapters 15, 16, 17] by C. S. Lewis, which will be published in the year 1964. This limited edition is published as a New Year's greeting to friends of the author and his publisher')

39 *Letters to Malcolm: Chiefly on Prayer* London: Geoffrey Bles Ltd, 1964

40 *The Discarded Image: An Introduction to Medieval and Renaissance Literature* Cambridge: Cambridge University Press, 1964

41 *Poems* (Edited by Walter Hooper). London: Geoffrey Bles Ltd, 1964

42 *Screwtape Proposes a Toast and Other Pieces* London: Fontana Books, 1965. (Contents: 'Screwtape Proposes a Toast', 'On Obstinacy in Belief', 'Good Work and Good Works', 'The Inner Ring', 'Is Theology Poetry?', 'Transposition' (an expanded version of the one published previously), 'The Weight of Glory', 'A Slip of the Tongue')

43 *Studies in Medieval and Renaissance Literature* (Collected by Walter Hooper). Cambridge: Cambridge University Press, 1966

44 *Letters of C. S. Lewis* (Edited by W. H. Lewis). Geoffrey Bles Ltd, 1966

B Short Stories

1 'The Shoddy Lands', *The Magazine of Fantasy and Science Fiction* (American), X (Feb. 1956), pp. 68–74. (Reprinted in *The Best from Fantasy and Science Fiction*. Sixth Series, Edited by Anthony Boucher, New York: Doubleday and Co., Inc., 1957, pp. 158–66)

2 'Ministering Angels', *The Magazine of Fantasy and Science Fiction* (American), XIII (Jan. 1958), pp. 5–14. (Reprinted in *The Best from Fantasy and Science Fiction*. Eighth Series, Edited by Anthony Boucher, New York: Doubleday and Co., Inc., 1959, pp. 13–24)

C Books edited or with Prefaces by C. S. Lewis

1 St Athanasius, *The Incarnation of the Word of God: Being the Treatise of St Athanasius 'De Incarnatione Verbi Dei'* with an Introduction by C. S. Lewis. (Translated and edited by A Religious of C.S.M.V. [R. P. Lawson].) London: Geoffrey Bles Ltd, 1944. Second edition entitled *St Athanasius on the Incarnation: The Treatise 'De Incarnatione Verbi Dei'* with an Introduction by C. S. Lewis, New Edition, revised, with a Letter of St Athanasius *On the Interpretation of the Psalms* added as an Appendix. London: A. R. Mowbray and Co. Ltd, 1953

2 C. S. Lewis, *George Macdonald: An Anthology* London: Geoffrey Bles Ltd, 1946. (Preface by C. S. Lewis and 365 brief excerpts from the works of George Macdonald)

3 B. G. Sandhurst, *How Heathen is Britain?* London: Collins, 1946. (Preface by C. S. Lewis.) Revised and Enlarged Edition, 1948

4 Eric Bentley, *The Cult of the Superman: A Study of the Idea of Heroism in Carlyle and Nietzsche, with Notes on Other*

Hero-Worshippers of Modern Times with an Appreciation by C. S. Lewis. London: Robert Hale Ltd, 1947

5 J. B. Phillips, *Letters to Young Churches: A Translation of the New Testament Epistles* with an Introduction by C. S. Lewis. London: Geoffrey Bles Ltd, 1947

6 Dorothy L. Sayers and others, *Essays Presented to Charles Williams* London, New York, Toronto: Oxford University Press, 1947. (With a Preface and an essay, 'On Stories', by C. S. Lewis)

7 C. S. Lewis, *Arthurian Torso: Containing the Posthumous Fragment of 'The Figure of Arthur' by Charles Williams and a Commentary on the Arthurian Poems of Charles Williams by C. S. Lewis* London, New York, Toronto: Oxford University Press, 1948

8 D. E. Harding, *The Hierarchy of Heaven and Earth: A New Diagram of Man in the Universe*, Preface by C. S. Lewis. London: Faber and Faber Ltd, 1952

9 Joy Davidman, *Smoke on the Mountain: An Interpretation of the Ten Commandments in Terms of To-day* London: Hodder and Stoughton Ltd, 1955. (With a Foreword by C. S. Lewis)

10 Austin Farrer, *A Faith of Our Own* with a Preface by C. S. Lewis. Cleveland and New York: World Publishing Co., 1960

11 Laʒamon, *Selections from Laʒamon's 'Brut'* with an Introduction by C. S. Lewis. (Edited by G. L. Brook.) Oxford: Clarendon Press, 1963

D Essays and Pamphlets

1 'The Expedition to Holly Bush Hill', *Cherbourg School Magazine*, (Nov. 1912)

2 'Are Athletes Better than Scholars?' *Cherbourg School Magazine*, No. 2, (1913)

3 'A Note on *Comus*', *The Review of English Studies*, VIII (April 1932) pp. 170–6

4 'What Chaucer really did to *Il Filostrato*', *Essays and Studies by Members of the English Association*, XVII (1932) pp. 56–75

5 'The Personal Heresy in Criticism', *Essays and Studies by Members of the English Association*, XIX (1934) pp. 7–28; cf. E. M. W. Tillyard, 'The Personal Heresy in Criticism: A Rejoinder', *ib.*, XX (1935) pp. 7–20; C. S. Lewis, 'Open Letter to Dr Tillyard', *ib.*, XXI (1936) pp. 153–68. (These three essays form the first half of *The Personal Heresy: A Controversy*)

6 'A Metrical Suggestion', *Lysistrata*, II (May 1935) pp. 13–24. (Reprinted as 'The Alliterative Metre' in *Rehabilitations and other Essays*)

7 'Genius and Genius', *The Review of English Studies*, XII (April 1936) pp. 189–94

8 'Donne and Love Poetry in the Seventeenth Century', *Seventeenth Century Studies Presented to Sir Herbert Grierson*. Oxford: Clarendon Press, 1938, pp. 64–84

9 'The Fifteenth Century Heroic Line,' *Essays and Studies by Members of the English Association*, XXIV (1939) pp. 28–41

10 'Christianity and Culture', *Theology*, XL (March 1940) pp. 166–79; cf. S. L. Bethell and E. F. Carritt, 'Christianity and Culture: Replies to Mr Lewis', *ib.*, XL (May 1940) pp. 356–66; C. S. Lewis, 'Christianity and Culture' (a letter), *ib.*, XL (June 1940) pp. 475–7; George Every, 'In Defence of Criticism', *ib.*, XLI (Sept. 1940) pp. 159–65; C. S. Lewis, 'Peace Proposals for Brother Every and Mr Bethell', *ib.*, XLI (Dec. 1940) pp. 339–48

11 'Dangers of National Repentance', *The Guardian*, (15 March 1940) p. 127

12 'Two Ways with the Self', *The Guardian*, (3 May 1940) p. 215

13 'Notes on the Way', *Time and Tide*, XXI (17 Aug. 1940) p. 841. (Reprinted as 'Importance of an Ideal', *Living Age*, CCCLIX (Oct. 1940) pp. 109–11)

14 'Meditation on the Third Commandment', *The Guardian*, (10 Jan. 1941) p. 18

15 'Evil and God', *The Spectator*, CLXVI (7 Feb. 1941) p. 141

16 'Edmund Spenser', *Fifteen Poets*. London: Oxford University Press, 1941, pp. 40–3

17 'Notes on the Way', *Time and Tide*, XXII (29 March 1941) p. 261. (Reprinted, and expanded, as ' "Bulverism", or, The Foundation of 20th Century Thought', *The Socratic Digest*, No. 2 (June 1944) pp. 16–20)

18 'The Screwtape Letters', *The Guardian*: (2 May 1941) pp. 211–2; (9 May 1941) pp. 223–4; (16 May 1941) pp. 235–6; (23 May 1941) pp. 246, 249; (30 May 1941), pp. 259–60; (6 June 1941) pp. 270, 273; (13 June 1941) p. 282; (20 June 1941) pp. 291–2; (27 June 1941) pp. 307–8; (4 July 1941) pp. 319–20; (11 July 1941) pp. 331–2; (18 July 1941) pp. 343–4; (25 July 1941) pp. 355–6; (1 Aug. 1941) pp. 367–8; (8 Aug. 1941) pp. 378, 382; (15 Aug. 1941) pp. 391–2; (22 Aug. 1941) p. 402; (29 Aug. 1941) pp. 417–8; (5 Sept. 1941) p. 426; (12 Sept. 1941) pp. 443–4; (19 Sept. 1941) pp. 451–2; (26 Sept. 1941) p. 465; (3 Oct. 1941) pp. 475–6; (10 Oct 1941) p. 490; (17 Oct. 1941) pp. 498, 502; (24 Oct. 1941) p. 514; (31 Oct. 1941) p. 526; (7 Nov. 1941) p. 531; (14 Nov. 1941) p. 550; (21 Nov. 1941) p. 558; (28 Nov. 1941) p. 570. (These instalments are published, with some alterations, in book-form as *The Screwtape Letters*)

19 'Religion: Reality or Substitute?' *World Dominion*, XIX (Sept.–Oct. 1941) pp. 277–81

20 'The Weight of Glory', *Theology*, XLIII (Nov. 1941) pp. 263–74

21 'Psycho-analysis and Literary Criticism', *Essays and Studies by Members of the English Association*, XXVII (1942) pp. 7–21

22 *Hamlet: The Prince or the Poem?* Annual Shakespeare Lecture of the British Academy, 1942, *The Proceedings of the British*

Academy, XXVIII, London: Oxford University Press, 1942, 18 pp.

23 'Notes on the Way', *Time and Tide*, XXIII (27 June 1942) pp. 519–20

24 'Miracles', *The Guardian*, (2 Oct. 1942) p. 316

25 'Miracles', *Saint Jude's Gazette*, No. 73 (Oct. 1942) pp. 4–7. (Published by St Jude on the Hill Church, Golders Green)

26 Preface to *The Socratic Digest*, No. 1 (1942–3) pp. 3–5

27 'Dogma and the Universe', *The Guardian*, (19 March 1943) p. 96

28 'The Poison of Subjectivism', *Religion in Life*, XII (Summer 1943) pp. 356–65

29 'Equality', *The Spectator*, CLXXI (27 Aug. 1943) p. 192

30 'Notes on the Way', *Time and Tide*, XXIV (4 Sept. 1943) p. 717

31 'Is English Doomed?' *The Spectator*, CLXXII (11 Feb. 1944) p. 121

32 'The Map and the Ocean', *The Listener*, XXXI (24 Feb. 1944) p. 216; 'God in Three Persons', *ib.* (2 March 1944) p. 244; 'The Whole Purpose of the Christian', *ib.* (9 March 1944) p. 272; 'The Obstinate Tin Soldiers', *ib.* (16 March 1944) p. 300; 'Let us Pretend', *ib.* (23 March 1944), p. 328; 'Is Christianity Hard or Easy?' *ib.* (30 March 1944) p. 356; 'The New Man', *ib.* (6 April 1944) p. 384. (These instalments are published, with some alterations, in book-form as *Beyond Personality: The Christian Idea of God*)

33 'Notes on the Way', *Time and Tide*, XXV (11 March 1944) p. 213

34 *Answers to Questions on Christianity*. Electric and Musical Industries Christian Fellowship, Hayes, Middlesex, [1944], 24 pp. (From the Preface: 'A "One Man Brains Trust" held on 18 April 1944, at the Head Office of Electric and Musical Industries, Ltd'. H. W. Bowen, Questionmaster)

I

35 'Notes on the Way', *Time and Tide*, XXV (29 April 1944) pp. 369–70

36 'A Dream', *The Spectator*, CLXXIII (28 July 1944) p. 77

37 'Blimpophobia', *Time and Tide*, XXV (9 Sept. 1944) p. 785

38 'The Death of Words', *The Spectator*, CLXXIII (22 Sept. 1944) p. 261

39 'Myth Became Fact', *World Dominion*, XXII (Sept.–Oct. 1944) pp. 267–70

40 'Horrid Red Things', *Church of England Newspaper*, LI (6 Oct. 1944) pp. 1–2

41 'Who Goes Home? or The Grand Divorce', *The Guardian:* (10 Nov. 1944) pp. 399–400; (17 Nov. 1944) pp. 411, 413; (24 Nov. 1944) pp. 421–2; (1 Dec. 1944) pp. 431–2; (8 Dec. 1944) pp. 442, 445; (15 Dec. 1944) pp. 453–4; (22 Dec. 1944) pp. 463–5; (29 Dec. 1944) pp. 472–4; (5 Jan. 1945) pp. 4, 8; (12 Jan. 1945) pp. 15, 18; (19 Jan. 1945) pp. 25–6; (26 Jan. 1945) pp. 34, 37; (2 Feb. 1945) pp. 45, 48; (9 Feb. 1945) p. 52; (16 Feb. 1945) pp. 63–4; (23 Feb. 1945) pp. 73, 77; (2 March 1945) p. 84; (9 March 1945) pp. 95–6; (16 March 1945) p. 104; (23 March 1945) pp. 114, 117; (29 March 1945) p. 124; (6 April 1945) p. 132; (13 April 1945) p. 141. (These instalments are published in book-form as *The Great Divorce: A Dream*)

42 'Private Bates', *The Spectator*, CLXXIII (29 Dec. 1944) p. 596

43 'Religion and Science', *The Coventry Evening Telegraph* (3 Jan. 1945) p. 4

44 'Who Was Right—Dream Lecturer or Real Lecturer?' *The Coventry Evening Telegraph* (21 Feb. 1945) p. 4

45 'The Laws of Nature', *The Coventry Evening Telegraph*, (4 April 1945) p. 4

46 'The Grand Miracle', *The Guardian*, (27 April 1945) pp. 161, 165

47 'Charles Walter Stansby Williams (1886–1945)', *The Oxford Magazine*, LXIII (24 May 1945) p. 265. (An obituary notice)

48 'Work and Prayer', *The Coventry Evening Telegraph*, (28 May 1945) p. 4

49 'Membership', *Sobornost*, No. 31, New Series (June 1945) pp. 4–9

50 'Hedonics', *Time and Tide*, XXVI (16 June 1945) pp. 494–5

51 'Oliver Elton (1861–1945)', *The Oxford Magazine*, LXIII (21 June 1945) pp. 318–19. (An obituary notice)

52 'Meditation in a Toolshed', *The Coventry Evening Telegraph*, (17 July 1945) p. 4

53 'Addison', *Essays on the Eighteenth Century Presented to David Nichol Smith* Oxford: Clarendon Press, 1945 pp. 1–14

54 'The Sermon and the Lunch', *Church of England Newspaper*, No. 2, 692 (21 Sept. 1945) pp. 1–2

55 'Scraps', *St James' Magazine*, (Dec. 1945) pp. [4–5]. (Published by St James' Church, Birkdale, Southport)

56 'After Priggery—What?' *The Spectator*, CLXXV (7 Dec. 1945) p. 536

57 'Is Theology Poetry?' *The Socratic Digest*, No. 3 (1945) pp. 25–35.

58 *Man or Rabbit?* Student Christian Movement in Schools, [n.d.], 4 pp. (A pamphlet, probably published in about 1946)

59 Sermon in *Five Sermons by Laymen*. S. Matthew's Church, Northampton, (April–May 1946) pp. 1–6. (Reprinted, with slight alterations, as '*Miserable Offenders*': *An Interpretation of Prayer Book Language*, Advent Paper No. 12. Boston: Church of the Advent [n.d.], 12 pp.)

60 'Notes on the Way', *Time and Tide*, XXVII (25 May 1946) p. 486

61 'Notes on the Way', *Time and Tide*, XXVII (1 June 1946) pp. 510–11

62 'Talking about Bicycles', *Resistance*, (Oct. 1946) pp. 10–13

63 'Notes on the Way', *Time and Tide*, XXVII (9 Nov. 1946) pp. 1070–1

64 'The Decline of Religion', *The Cherwell*, XXVI (29 Nov. 1946) pp. 8–10

65 'A Christian Reply to Professor Price', *Phoenix Quarterly*, I, No. 1 (Autumn 1946) pp. 31–44; cf. H. H. Price, 'The Grounds of Modern Agnosticism', *ib.*, pp. 10–30

66 'On Stories', *Essays Presented to Charles Williams* London: Oxford University Press, 1947, pp. 90–105

67 *Vivisection*, [with portrait], and a Foreword by George R. Farnum. Boston: New England Anti-Vivisection Society, [1947] 11 pp. (Reprinted (with portrait), and a Foreword by R. Fielding-Ould. London: National Anti-Vivisection Society, [1948] 11 pp.)

68 'Kipling's World', *Literature and Life: Addresses to the English Association*, *I*. London: Harrap and Co., 1948, pp. 57–73

69 'Some Thoughts', *The First Decade: Ten Years' Work of the Medical Missionaries of Mary*. Dublin: At the Sign of the Three Candles, [1948] pp. 91–4

70 'Religion without Dogma?' *The Socratic Digest*, No. 4 [1948] pp. 82–94; cf. H. H. Price, 'Reply', *ib.*, pp. 94–102; G. E. M. Anscombe, 'A Reply to Mr C. S. Lewis' Argument that "Naturalism" is Self-refuting', *ib.*, pp. 7–15; C. S. Lewis, 'Reply', *ib.*, pp. 15–16

71 'The Trouble with "X" . . .', *Bristol Diocesan Gazette*, XXVII (Aug. 1948) pp. 3–6

72 'Notes on the Way', *Time and Tide*, XXIX (14 Aug. 1948) pp. 830–1

73 'Difficulties in Presenting the Christian Faith to Modern Unbelievers', (English text with French translation), *Lumen Vitae*, III (Sept. 1948) pp. 421–6

74 'On Church Music', *English Church Music*, XIX (April 1949) pp. 19–22

75 'The Humanitarian Theory of Punishment', *20th Century: An Australian Quarterly Review*, III, No. 3 (1949) pp. 5–12; cf. Norval Morris and Donald Buckle, 'A Reply to C. S. Lewis', *ib.*, VI, No. 2 (1952) pp. 20–6

These two articles are reprinted in *Res Judicatae*, VI (June 1953) pp. 224–30 and pp. 231–7 respectively

The controversy continues with the following articles: J. J. C. Smart, 'Comment: The Humanitarian Theory of Punishment', *Res Judicatae*, VI (Feb. 1954) pp. 368–71; C. S. Lewis, 'On Punishment: A Reply', *ib.*, (Aug. 1954) pp. 519–23

76 (With C. E. M. Joad) 'The Pains of Animals: A Problem in Theology', *The Month*, CLXXXIX (Feb. 1950) pp. 95–104.

77 *The Literary Impact of the Authorised Version* The Ethel M. Wood Lecture delivered before the University of London on 20 March 1950. London: The Athlone Press, 1950, 26 pp.

78 'Historicism', *The Month*, IV (Oct. 1950) pp. 230–43

79 (With Arnold Toynbee and Amos Wilder) 'Christian Hope —Its Meaning for Today', *Religion in Life*, XXI (Winter, 1951–52), pp. 20–32. (Reprinted as 'The World's Last Night' in *The World's Last Night and Other Essays*)

80 *Hero and Leander*, Warton Lecture on English Poetry, British Academy, 1952. *The Proceedings of the British Academy*, XXXVIII, London: Oxford University Press [1952] 37 pp.

81 'Is Theism Important? A Reply', *The Socratic [Digest]*, No. 5 (1952) pp. 48–51; cf. H. H. Price, 'Is Theism Important?' *ib.*, pp. 39–47

82 'On Three Ways of Writing for Children', *Library Association. Proceedings, Papers and Summaries of Discussions at the Bournemouth Conference 29 April to 2 May 1952* London: Library Association (1952) pp. 22–8

83 'Edmund Spenser', *Major British Writers, Vol. I.* (Edited by G. B. Harrison), New York: Harcourt, Brace and Co., 1954, pp. 91–103

84 'A Note on Jane Austen', *Essays in Criticism*, IV (Oct. 1954) pp. 359–71

85 'Xmas and Christmas: A Lost Chapter from Herodotus', *Time and Tide*, XXXV (4 Dec. 1954) p. 1607

86 'George Orwell', *Time and Tide*, XXXVI (8 Jan. 1955) pp. 43–4

87 'Prudery and Philology', *The Spectator*, CXCIV (21 Jan. 1955) pp. 63–4

88 *De Descriptione Temporum*, An Inaugural Lecture by the Professor of Medieval and Renaissance English Literature in the University of Cambridge. Cambridge: Cambridge University Press, 1955, 22 pp.

89 'Lilies that Fester', *Twentieth Century*, CLVII (April 1955) pp. 330–41

90 'On Obstinacy in Belief', *The Sewanee Review*, LXIII (Autumn 1955) pp. 525–38

91 [A toast to] 'The Memory of Sir Walter Scott', *The Edinburgh Sir Walter Scott Club Forty-ninth Annual Report, 1956*. Edinburgh, 1956, pp. 13–25. (Reprinted as 'Sir Walter Scott' in *They Asked for a Paper: Papers and Addresses*)

92 'Critical Forum: *De Descriptione Temporum*', *Essays in Criticism*, VI (April 1956) p. 247

93 'Interim Report', *The Cambridge Review*, (21 April 1956) pp. 468–71

94 'Sometimes Fairy Stories May Say Best What's to be Said', *The New York Times Book Review, Children's Book Section*, (18 Nov. 1956), p. 3

95 'Behind the Scenes', *Time and Tide*, XXXVII (1 Dec. 1956) pp. 1450–1

96 'Is History Bunk?' *The Cambridge Review*, LXXVIII (1 June 1957) pp. 647, 649

97 'Dante's Statius', *Medium Aevum*, XXV, No. 3 (1957) pp. 133–9

98 'What Christmas Means to Me', *Twentieth Century*, CLXII (Dec. 1957) pp. 517–18

99 'Delinquents in the Snow', *Time and Tide*, XXXVIII (7 Dec. 1957) pp. 1521–2

100 'Will We Lose God in Outer Space?' *Christian Herald*, LXXXI (April 1958) pp. 19, 74–6. (Reprinted as *Shall We Lose God in Outer Space?* London: SPCK, 1959, 11 pp. Appears as 'Religion and Rocketry' in *The World's Last Night and Other Essays*)

101 'Revival or Decay?' *Punch*, CCXXXV (9 July 1958) pp. 36–8

102 'Is Progress Possible?—2: Willing Slaves of the Welfare State', *The Observer*, (20 July 1958) p. 6; cf. C. P. Snow, 'Is Progress Possible?—1: Man in Society', *ib*. (13 July 1958) p. 12

103 'Rejoinder to Dr Pittenger', *The Christian Century*, LXXV (26 Nov. 1958) pp. 1359–61; cf. W. Norman Pittenger, 'Apologist Versus Apologist: A Critique of C. S. Lewis as "defender of the faith"', *ib*., LXXV (1 Oct. 1958) pp. 1104–7

104 'On Juvenile Tastes', *Church Times, Children's Book Supplement*, (28 Nov. 1958), p. i

105 'The Efficacy of Prayer', *The Atlantic Monthly*, CCIII (Jan 1959) pp. 59–61

106 'Screwtape Proposes a Toast', *The Saturday Evening Post*, CCXXXII (19 Dec. 1959) pp. 36, 86, 88–9

107 'Good Work and Good Works', *Good Work*, XXIII (Christmas 1959) pp. 3–10

108 'Metre', *A Review of English Literature*, I (Jan. 1960), pp. 45–50

109 'Undergraduate Criticism', *Broadsheet* (Cambridge), VIII, No. 17 (9 March 1960)

110 'It All Began with a Picture . . .', *Radio Times, Junior Radio Times*, CXLVIII (15 July 1960)

111 'Haggard Rides Again', *Time and Tide*, XLI (3 Sept. 1960) pp. 1044–5

112 'Four-letter Words', *The Critical Quarterly*, III (Summer 1961) pp. 118–22

113 'Before We Can Communicate', *Breakthrough*, No. 8 (Oct. 1961) p. 2

114 'The Anthropological Approach', *English and Medieval Studies Presented to J. R. R. Tolkien on the Occasion of his Seventieth Birthday*. Edited by Norman Davis and C. L. Wrenn. London: George Allen and Unwin Ltd, 1962, pp. 219–30

115 'Sex in Literature', *The Sunday Telegraph*, No. 87 (30 Sept. 1962) p. 8

116 'The Vision of John Bunyan', *The Listener*, LXVIII (13 Dec. 1962) pp. 1006–8

117 'Going into Europe: A Symposium', *Encounter*, XIX (Dec. 1962) p. 57

118 'The English Prose "Morte"', *Essays on Malory*. Edited by J. A. W. Bennett. Oxford: Clarendon Press, 1963, pp. 7–28

119 'Onward, Christian Spacemen', *Show*, III (Feb. 1963) pp. 57, 117

120 'Must Our Image of God Go?' *The Observer* (24 March 1963) p. 14; cf. The Bishop of Woolwich, 'Our Image of God Must Go', *ib.* (17 March 1963) p. 21

(Lewis's article is reprinted in *The Honest to God Debate: Some Reactions to the Book 'Honest to God' with a new chapter by its author, John A. T. Robinson, Bishop of Woolwich*. Edited by David L. Edwards, London: SCM Press Ltd, 1963, p. 91)

121 'I Was Decided Upon', *Decision*, II (Sept. 1963) p. 3. (Answers to questions when interviewed by Sherwood E. Wirt of the Billy Graham Evangelistic Association Ltd)

122 'Heaven, Earth and Outer Space', *Decision*, II (Oct. 1963) p. 4. (Answers to questions when interviewed by Sherwood E. Wirt of the Billy Graham Evangelistic Association Ltd)

123 'We Have No "Right to Happiness"', *The Saturday Evening Post*, CCXXXVI (21–8 Dec. 1963) pp. 10, 12

124 '"The establishment must die and rot . . . ": C. S. Lewis Discusses Science Fiction with Kingsley Amis', *SF Horizons*, No. 1 (Spring 1964) pp. 5–12. (An informal conversation recorded on tape by Brian Aldiss in Lewis's rooms in Magdalene College, Cambridge, 1963)

E Poems

(Lewis wrote most of his poems over the pseudonym, Nat Whilk, or the initials, N.W., as marked in this section. Even though many were revised and given new titles by the author, all the following appear in *Poems*, with the exception of Nos. 1, 2, 3, 17, 19, and 58.)

1 '*Quam Bene Saturno*', *Cherbourg School Magazine* (29 July 1913)

2 'Death in Battle', *Reveille*, No. 3 (Feb. 1919) p. 508 (Clive Hamilton). (Reprinted in *Spirits in Bondage: A Cycle of Lyrics*)

3 (With A. Owen Barfield) 'Abecedarium Philosophicum', *The Oxford Magazine*, LII (30 Nov. 1933) p. 298

4 'The Shortest Way Home', *The Oxford Magazine*, LII (10 May 1934) p. 665 (Nat Whilk). (Revised and re-titled 'Man is a Lumpe Where All Beasts Kneaded Be' in *Poems*)

5 'Scholar's Melancholy', *The Oxford Magazine*, LII (24 May 1934) p. 734 (Nat Whilk)

6 'The Planets', *Lysistrata*, II (May 1935) pp. 21–4. (Forms part of the essay, 'A Metrical Suggestion')

7 'Sonnet', *The Oxford Magazine*, LIV (14 May 1936) p. 575 (Nat Whilk)

8 'Coronation March', *The Oxford Magazine*, LV (6 May 1937) p. 565 (Nat Whilk)

9 'After Kirby's *Kalevala*', (a translation), *The Oxford Magazine*, LV (13 May 1937) p. 595 (Nat Whilk)

10 'The Future of Forestry', *The Oxford Magazine*, LVI (10 Feb 1938) p. 383 (Nat Whilk)

11 '*Chanson D'Aventure*', *The Oxford Magazine*, LVI (19 May 1938) p. 638 (Nat Whilk). (Revised and re-titled 'What the Bird Said Early in the Year' in *Poems*)

12 'Experiment', *The Spectator*, CLXI (9 Dec. 1938) p. 998. (Revised and re-titled 'Pattern' in *Poems*)

13 'To Mr Roy Campbell', *The Cherwell*, LVI (6 May 1939) p. 35 (Nat Whilk). (Revised and re-titled 'To the Author of *Flowering Rifle*' in *Poems*)

14 'Hermione in the House of Paulina', *Augury: An Oxford Miscellany of Verse and Prose*. Edited by Alec M. Hardie and Keith C. Douglas, Oxford: Basil Blackwell, 1940, p. 28. (Revised in *Poems*)

15 'Epitaph', *Time and Tide*, XXIII (6 June 1942) p. 460 (Re-titled 'Epigrams and Epitaphs, No. 11' in *Poems*)

16 'To G.M.', *The Spectator*, CLXIX (9 Oct. 1942) p. 335. (Revised and re-titled 'To a Friend' in *Poems*)

17 'Awake, My Lute!' *The Atlantic Monthly*, CLXXII (Nov. 1943) pp. 113, 115

18 'The Salamander', *The Spectator*, CLXXIV (8 June 1945) p. 521. See erratum: 'Poet and Printer', *ib.* (15 June 1945) p. 550

19 'From the Latin of Milton's *De Idea Platonica Quemadmodum Aristoteles Intellexit*' (a translation), *English*, V, No. 30 (1945) p. 195

20 'On the Death of Charles Williams', *Britain To-day*, No. 112 (Aug. 1945) p. 14. (Revised and re-titled 'To Charles Williams' in *Poems*)

21 'Under Sentence', *The Spectator*, CLXXV (7 Sept. 1945)

p. 219. (Revised and re-titled 'The Condemned' in *Poems*)

22 'On the Atomic Bomb (Metrical Experiment)', *The Spectator*, CLXXV (28 Dec. 1945) p. 619

23 'On Receiving Bad News', *Time and Tide*, XXVI (29 Dec. 1945) p. 1093. (Re-titled 'Epigrams and Epitaphs, No. 12' in *Poems*)

24 'The Birth of Language', *Punch*, CCX (9 Jan. 1946) p. 32 (N.W.). (Revised in *Poems*)

25 'On Being Human', *Punch*, CCX (8 May 1946) p. 402 (N.W.). (Revised in *Poems*)

26 'Solomon', *Punch*, CCXI (14 Aug. 1946) p. 136 (N.W.). (Revised in *Poems*)

27 'The True Nature of Gnomes', *Punch*, CCXI (16 Oct. 1946) p. 310 (N.W.)

28 'The Meteorite', *Time and Tide*, XXVII (7 Dec. 1946) p. 1183

29 'Pan's Purge', *Punch*, CCXII (15 Jan. 1947) p. 71 (N.W.)

30 'The Romantics', *The New English Weekly*, XXX (16 Jan. 1947) p. 130. (Revised and re-titled 'The Prudent Jailer' in *Poems*)

31 'Dangerous Oversight', *Punch*, CCXII (21 May 1947) p. 434 (N.W.). (Revised and re-titled 'Young King Cole' in *Poems*)

32 'Two Kinds of Memory', *Time and Tide*, XXVIII (7 Aug. 1947) p. 859. (Revised in *Poems*)

33 '*Le Roi S'Amuse*', *Punch*, CCXIII (1 Oct. 1947) p. 324 (N.W.). (Revised in *Poems*)

34 'Donkeys' Delight', *Punch*, CCXIII (5 Nov. 1947) p. 442 (N.W.). (Revised in *Poems*)

35 'The End of the Wine', *Punch*, CCXIII (3 Dec. 1947) p. 538 (N.W.). (Revised and re-titled 'The Last of the Wine' in *Poems*)

36 'Vitrea Circe', *Punch*, CCXIV (23 June 1948) p. 543 (N.W.). (Revised in *Poems*)

37 'Epitaph', *The Spectator*, CLXXXI (30 July 1948) p. 142. (Revised and re-titled 'Epigrams and Epitaphs, No. 14' in *Poems*)

38 'The Sailing of the Ark', *Punch*, CCXV (11 Aug. 1948) p. 124 (N.W.). (Revised and re-titled 'The Late Passenger' in *Poems*)

39 'The Landing', *Punch*, CCXV (15 Sept. 1948) p. 237 (N.W.). (Revised in *Poems*)

40 'The Turn of the Tide', *Punch* (Almanac), CCXV (1 Nov. 1948) (N.W.). (Revised in *Poems*)

41 'The Prodigality of Firdausi', *Punch*, CCXV (1 Dec. 1948) p. 510 (N.W.). (Revised in *Poems*)

42 'Epitaph in a Village Churchyard', *Time and Tide*, XXX (19 March 1949) p. 272. (Re-titled 'Epigrams and Epitaphs, No. 16' in *Poems*)

43 'On a Picture by Chirico', *The Spectator*, CLXXXII (6 May 1949) p. 607. (Revised in *Poems*)

44 'Adam at Night', *Punch*, CCXVI (11 May 1949) p. 510 (N.W.). (Revised and re-titled 'The Adam at Night' in *Poems*)

45 'Arrangement of Pindar', *Mandrake*, I, No. 6 (1949) pp. 43–5. (Revised and re-titled 'Pindar Sang' in *Poems*)

46 'Epitaph', *The Month*, II (July 1949) p. 8. (Re-titled 'Epigrams and Epitaphs, No. 17' in *Poems*)

47 'Conversation Piece: The Magician and the Dryad', *Punch*, CCXVII (20 July 1949) p. 71 (N.W.). (Revised and re-titled 'The Magician and the Dryad' in *Poems*)

48 'The Day with a White Mark', *Punch*, CCXVII (17 Aug. 1949) p. 170 (N.W.). (Revised in *Poems*)

49 'A Footnote to Pre-History', *Punch*, CCXVII (14 Sept. 1949) p. 304 (N.W.). (Revised and re-titled 'The Adam Unparadised' in *Poems*)

50 'As One Oldster to Another', *Punch*, CCXVIII (15 March 1950) pp. 294–5 (N.W.). (Revised in *Poems*)

51 'A Cliché Came Out of its Cage', *Nine: A Magazine of Poetry and Criticism*, II (May 1950) p. 114. (Revised in *Poems*)

52 'Ballade of Dead Gentlemen', *Punch*, CCXX (28 March 1951) p. 386 (N.W.)

53 'The Country of the Blind', *Punch*, CCXXI (12 Sept. 1951) p. 303 (N.W.)

54 'Pilgrim's Problem', *The Month*, VII (May 1952) p. 275

55 'Vowels and Sirens', *The Times Literary Supplement*, Special Autumn Issue, (29 Aug. 1952) p. xiv. (Revised in *Poems*)

56 'Impenitence', *Punch*, CCXXV (15 July 1953) p. 91 (N.W.)

57 'March for Drum, Trumpet and Twenty-one Giants', *Punch*, CCXXV (4 Nov. 1953) p. 553 (N.W.). (Revised in *Poems*)

58 'To Mr Kingsley Amis on His Late Verses', *Essays in Criticism*, IV (April 1954) p. 190; cf. Kingsley Amis, 'Beowulf', *ib.* (Jan. 1954) p. 85

59 '*Odora Canum Vis* (A defence of certain modern biographers and critics)', *The Month*, XI (May 1954), p. 272. (Revised in *Poems*)

60 'Cradle-Song Based on a Theme from Nicolas of Cusa', *The Times Literary Supplement*, (11 June 1954) p. 375. (Revised and re-titled 'Science-Fiction Cradlesong' in *Poems*)

61 '*Spartan Nactus*', *Punch*, CCXXVII (1 Dec. 1954) p. 685 (N.W.). (Revised and re-titled 'A Confession' in *Poems*)

62 'On Another Theme from Nicolas of Cusa', *The Times Literary Supplement*, (21 Jan. 1955) p. 43. (Revised and re-titled 'On a Theme from Nicolas of Cusa' in *Poems*)

63 'Legion', *The Month*, XIII (April 1955) p. 210. (Revised in *Poems*)

64 'After Aristotle', *The Oxford Magazine*, LXXIV (23 Feb. 1956) p. 296 (N.W.)

65 'Epanorthosis (for the end of Goethe's *Faust*)', *The Cambridge Review*, LXXVII (26 May 1956) p. 610 (Nat Whilk). (Revised and re-titled 'Epigrams and Epitaphs, No. 15' in *Poems*)

66 'Evolutionary Hymn', *The Cambridge Review*, LXXIX (30 Nov. 1957) p. 227 (N.W.)

67 'An Expostulation (against too many writers of science fiction)', *The Magazine of Fantasy and Science Fiction*, XVI (June 1959) p. 47

F Book reviews by C. S. Lewis

(Some reviews were given titles. Whenever this occurs the title follows the name of the book reviewed.)

1 Hugh Kingsmill, *Matthew Arnold*. *The Oxford Magazine*, XLVII (15 Nov. 1928) p. 177

2 W. P. Ker, *Form and Style in Poetry*, (Edited by R. W. Chambers). *The Oxford Magazine*, XLVII (6 Dec. 1928) pp. 283–4

3 H. W. Garrod, *Collins*. *The Oxford Magazine*, XLVII (16 May 1929) p. 633

4 Ruth Mohl, *The Three Estates in Medieval and Renaissance Literature*. *Medium Aevum*, III (Feb. 1934) pp. 68–70

5 E. K. Chambers, *Sir Thomas Wyatt and Some Collected Studies*. *Medium Aevum*, III (Oct. 1934) pp. 237–40

6 T. R. Henn, *Longinus and English Criticism*. *The Oxford Magazine*, LIII (6 Dec. 1934) p. 264

7 Charles Williams, *Taliessin Through Logres*. 'A Sacred Poem', *Theology*, XXXVIII (April 1939) pp. 268–76

8 A. C. Bouquet (Editor), *A Lectionary of Christian Prose from the Second Century to the Twentieth Century*. *Theology*, XXXIX (Dec. 1939) pp. 467–8

9 D. de Rougemont, *Passion and Society* (Translated by M. Belgion); Claude Chavasse, *The Bride of Christ*. *Theology*, XL (June 1940) pp. 459–61

10 Lord David Cecil (Editor), *The Oxford Book of Christian Verse. The Review of English Studies*, XVII (Jan. 1941) pp. 95–102

11 Helen M. Barrett, *Boethius: Some Aspects of His Times and Work. Medium Aevum*, X (Feb. 1941) pp. 29–34

12 Logan Pearsall Smith, *Milton and His Modern Critics. The Cambridge Review*, (21 Feb. 1941) p. 280

13 Dorothy L. Sayers, *The Mind of the Maker. Theology*, XLIII (Oct. 1941) pp. 248–9

14 Andreas Capellanus, *The Art of Courtly Love* (with Introduction, translation, and notes by John Jay Parry). *The Review of English Studies*, XIX (Jan. 1943) pp. 77–9

15 J. W. H. Atkins, *English Literary Criticism: The Medieval Phase. The Oxford Magazine*, LXII (10 Feb. 1944) p. 158

16 Charles Williams, *Taliessin Through Logres. The Oxford Magazine*, LXIV (14 March 1946) pp. 248–50

17 Douglas Bush, *'Paradise Lost' in Our Time: Some Comments. The Oxford Magazine*, LXV (13 Feb. 1947) pp. 215–17

18 Sir Thomas Malory, *The Works of Sir Thomas Malory* (Edited by E. Vinaver). 'The Morte Darthur', *The Times Literary Supplement*, (7 June 1947) pp. 273–4. (Unsigned)

19 G. A. L. Burgeon, *This Ever Diverse Pair*. 'Life Partners', *Time and Tide*, XXXI (25 March 1950) p. 286

20 Howard Rollin Patch, *The Other World, According to Descriptions in Mediaeval Literature. Medium Aevum*. XX (1951) pp. 93–4

21 Alan M. F. Gunn, *The Mirror of Love: A Reinterpretation of 'The Romance of the Rose'. Medium Aevum*, XXII, No. 1 (1953) pp. 27–31

22 J. R. R. Tolkien, *The Fellowship of the Ring* (being the First Part of *The Lord of the Rings*). 'The Gods Return to Earth', *Time and Tide*, XXXV (14 Aug. 1954) pp. 1082–3

23 J. R. R. Tolkien, *The Two Towers* (being the Second Part of *The Lord of the Rings*); *The Return of the King* (being the

Third Part of *The Lord of the Rings*). 'The Dethronement of Power', *Time and Tide*, XXXVI (22 Oct. 1955) pp. 1373–4

24 W. Schwarz, *Principles and Problems of Biblical Translation*. *Medium Aevum*, XXVI, No. 2 (1957) pp. 115–17

25 R. S. Loomis (Editor), *Arthurian Literature in the Middle Ages: A Collaborative Study*. 'Arthuriana', *The Cambridge Review*, LXXXI (13 Feb. 1960) pp. 355, 357

26 M. Pauline Parker, *The Allegory of the 'Fairie Queen'*. *The Cambridge Review*, LXXXI (11 June 1960) pp. 643, 645

27 John Vyvyan, *Shakespeare and the Rose of Love*. *The Listener*, LXIV (7 July 1960) p. 30

28 Robert Ellrodt, *Neoplatonism in the Poetry of Spenser*. *Études Anglaises*, XIV (April–June 1961) pp. 107–16

29 George Steiner, *The Death of Tragedy*. 'Tragic Ends', *Encounter*, XVIII (Feb. 1962) pp. 97–101

30 Sir John Hawkins, *The Life of Samuel Johnson* (Edited by B. H. Davis). 'Boswell's Bugbear', *Sunday Telegraph*, No. 61 (1 April 1962) p. 8

31 Homer, *The Odyssey* (Translated by Robert Fitzgerald). 'Odysseus Sails Again', *Sunday Telegraph*, No. 84 (9 Sept. 1962) p. 6

32 John Jones, *On Aristotle and Greek Tragedy*. 'Ajax and Others', *Sunday Telegraph*, No. 98 (16 Dec. 1962) p. 6

33 Harold Bloom, *The Visionary Company: A Reading of English Romantic Poetry*. 'Poetry and Exegesis', *Encounter*, XX (June 1963) pp. 74–6

34 Dorothy L. Sayers, *The Poetry of Search and the Poetry of Statement*. 'Rhyme and Reason', *Sunday Telegraph*, No. 148 (1 Dec. 1963) p. 18

G Published Letters

1 'The Kingis Quair', *The Times Literary Supplement* (18 April 1929) p. 315

2 'Spenser's Irish Experiences and *The Faerie Queene*', *The Review of English Studies*, VII (Jan. 1931) pp. 83–5

3 'The Genuine Text', *The Times Literary Supplement*, (2 May 1935) p. 288; cf. J. Dover Wilson, *ib.* (16 May 1935) p. 313; C. S. Lewis, *ib.* (23 May 1935) p. 331; J. Dover Wilson, *ib.* (30 May 1935) p. 348; J. Dover Wilson, *ib.* (13 June 1935) p. 380

4 'The Conditions for a Just War', *Theology*, XXXVIII (May 1939) pp. 373–4

5 'Christianity and Culture', *Theology*, XL (June 1940) pp. 475–7

6 'The Conflict in Anglican Theology', *Theology*, XLI (Nov. 1940) p. 304

7 Open Letter, *The Christian News-Letter*, No. 119 (4 Feb. 1942) p. 4

8 'Miracles', *The Guardian*, (16 Oct. 1942) p. 331

9 Letter to the Publisher on dust cover of C. S. Lewis, *Perelandra*. New York: Macmillan Co., 1944

10 'Mr C. S. Lewis on Christianity', *The Listener*, XXXI (9 March 1944) p. 273; cf. W. R. Childe, *ib.* (2 March 1944) p. 245; W. R. Childe, *ib.* (16 March 1944) p. 301

11 'Basic Fears', *The Times Literary Supplement* (2 Dec. 1944) p. 583; S. H. Hooke, *ib.* (27 Jan. 1945) p. 43; C. S. Lewis, *ib.* (3 Feb. 1945) p. 55; S. H. Hooke, *ib.* (10 Feb. 1945) p. 67

12 'Above the Smoke and Stir', *The Times Literary Supplement* (14 July 1945) p. 331; cf. B. A. Wright, *ib.* (4 Aug. 1945) p. 367; C. S. Lewis, *ib.* (29 Sept. 1945) p. 463; B. A. Wright, *ib.* (27 Oct. 1945) p. 511

13 'A Village Experience', *The Guardian* (31 Aug. 1945) p. 335

14 'Socratic Wisdom', *The Oxford Magazine*, LXIV (13 June 1946) p. 359

15 'Poetic Licence', *The Sunday Times* (11 Aug. 1946) p. 6

16 'A Difference of Outlook', *The Guardian* (27 June 1947) p.

283; cf. A Correspondent, 'Adult Colleges', *ib.* (30 May 1947) pp. 235, 240

17 'Public Schools', *Church Times*, CXXX (3 Oct. 1947) p. 583

18 'The New Miltonians', *The Times Literary Supplement* (29 Nov. 1947) p. 615

19 (With Eric Routley) 'Correspondence with an Anglican who Dislikes Hymns', *The Presbyter*, VI, No. 2 (1948) pp. 15–20. (The two letters from Lewis, dated 16 July 1946 and 21 Sept. 1946, are printed over the initials 'A.B.')

20 'Charles Williams', *The Oxford Magazine*, LXVI (29 April 1948) p. 380

21 'Othello', *The Times Literary Supplement*, (19 June 1948) p. 345

22 'The Church's Liturgy', *Church Times*, CXXXII (20 May 1949) p. 319; cf. E. L. Mascall, 'Quadringentesimo Anno', *ib.* (6 May 1949) p. 282; W. D. F. Hughes, 'The Church's Liturgy', *ib.* (24 June 1949) p. 409; C. S. Lewis, *ib.* (1 July 1949) p. 427; Edward Every, 'Doctrine and Liturgy', *ib.* (8 July 1949) pp. 445–6; C. S. Lewis, 'Invocation', *ib.* (15 July 1949) pp. 463–4; Edward Every, 'Invocation of Saints', *ib.* (22 July 1949) pp. 481–2; C. S. Lewis, *ib.* (5 Aug. 1949) p. 513

23 'Text Corruptions', *The Times Literary Supplement*, (3 March 1950) p. 137; cf. J. Dover Wilson, *ib.* (10 March 1950) p. 153

24 Letter on '*Robinson Crusoe* as a Myth', *Essays in Criticism*, I (July 1951) p. 313; cf. Ian Watt, '*Robinson Crusoe* as a Myth', *ib.* (April 1951) pp. 95–119; Ian Watt, *ib.* (July 1951) p. 313

25 'The Holy Name', *Church Times*, CXXXIV (10 Aug. 1951) p. 541; cf. Leslie E. T. Bradbury, *ib.* (3 Aug. 1951) p. 525

26 'Mere Christians', *Church Times*, CXXXV (8 Feb. 1952) p. 95; R. D. Daunton-Fear, 'Evangelical Churchmanship', *ib.* (1 Feb. 1952) p. 77

27 'The Sheepheard's Slumber', *The Times Literary Supplement*, (9 May 1952) p. 313

28 'Canonization', *Church Times*, CXXXV (24 Oct. 1952) p. 763; cf. Eric Pitt, *ib.* (17 Oct. 1952) p. 743

29 Letter to the Publisher on dust cover of J. R. R. Tolkien, *The Fellowship of the Ring*. London: George Allen and Unwin Ltd, 1954

30 Letter to the Publisher on dust cover of A. C. Clarke, *Childhood's End*. London: Sidgwick and Jackson, 1954

31 Letter to the Milton Society of America, *A Milton Evening in Honor of Douglas Bush and C. S. Lewis*. Modern Language Association, (28 Dec. 1954) pp. 14–5

32 Open letter to Fr Berlicche, *L'Amico dei Buoni Fanciulli*, No. 1 (1955), Verona, p. 75

33 (With Dorothy L. Sayers) 'Charles Williams', *The Times*, (14 May 1955) p. 9

34 'Portrait of W. B. Yeats', *The Listener*, LIV (15 Sept. 1955) p. 427

35 Letter to the Publisher on dust cover of C. S. Lewis, *Till We Have Faces: A Myth Retold*. London: Geoffrey Bles Ltd, 1956

36 (With others) 'Mgr. R. A. Knox', *Church Times*, CXLI (6 June 1958) p. 12

37 'Books for Children', *The Times Literary Supplement* (28 Nov. 1958) p. 689; cf. 'The Light Fantastic', *ib.*, *Children's Books Section*, (21 Nov. 1958) p. x

38 Letter to the Publisher on dust cover of Mervyn Peake, *Titus Alone*. London: Eyre and Spottiswoode, 1959

39 Letter to the Publisher on dust cover of David Bolt, *Adam*. London: J. M. Dent and Sons, 1960

40 Letter to the Editor, *Delta: The Cambridge Literary Magazine*, No. 23 (Feb. 1961) pp. 4–7; cf. The Editors, 'Professor C. S. Lewis and the English Faculty', *ib.*, No. 22 (Oct. 1960) pp. 6–17; C. S. Lewis, 'Undergraduate Criticism', *Broadsheet* (Cambridge), VIII, No. 17 (9 March 1960)

41 Letters to 'A Member of the Church of the Covenant', quoted in the pamphlet, *Encounter with Light*. Lynchburg, Virginia: Church of the Covenant, [June 1961] pp. 11–16, 20. (The three letters from C. S. Lewis were written [14 Dec. 1950; 23 Dec. 1950; 17 April 1951] respectively)

42 'Capital Punishment', *Church Times*, CXLIV (1 Dec. 1961) p. 7; cf. Claude Davis, *ib.* (8 Dec. 1961) p. 14; C. S. Lewis, 'Death Penalty', *ib.* (15 Dec. 1961) p. 12

43 'And Less Greek', *Church Times*, CXLV (20 July 1962) p. 12

44 Letter to the Editor, *English*, XIV (Summer 1962), p. 75

45 'Wain's Oxford', *Encounter*, XX (Jan. 1963) p. 81

46 Letter quoted in Rose Macaulay, *Letters to a Sister* (Edited by Constance Babington Smith). London: Collins, 1964, p. 261 n. (Quotations from a letter C. S. Lewis wrote to Dorothea Conybeare, who had asked him to explain the title of his book, *Till We Have Faces*)

47 Letter to the Publisher on flyleaf of Austin Farrer, *Saving Belief: A Discussion of Essentials*. London: Hodder and Stoughton Ltd, 1964

AN ALPHABETICAL INDEX OF THE WRITINGS OF C. S. LEWIS